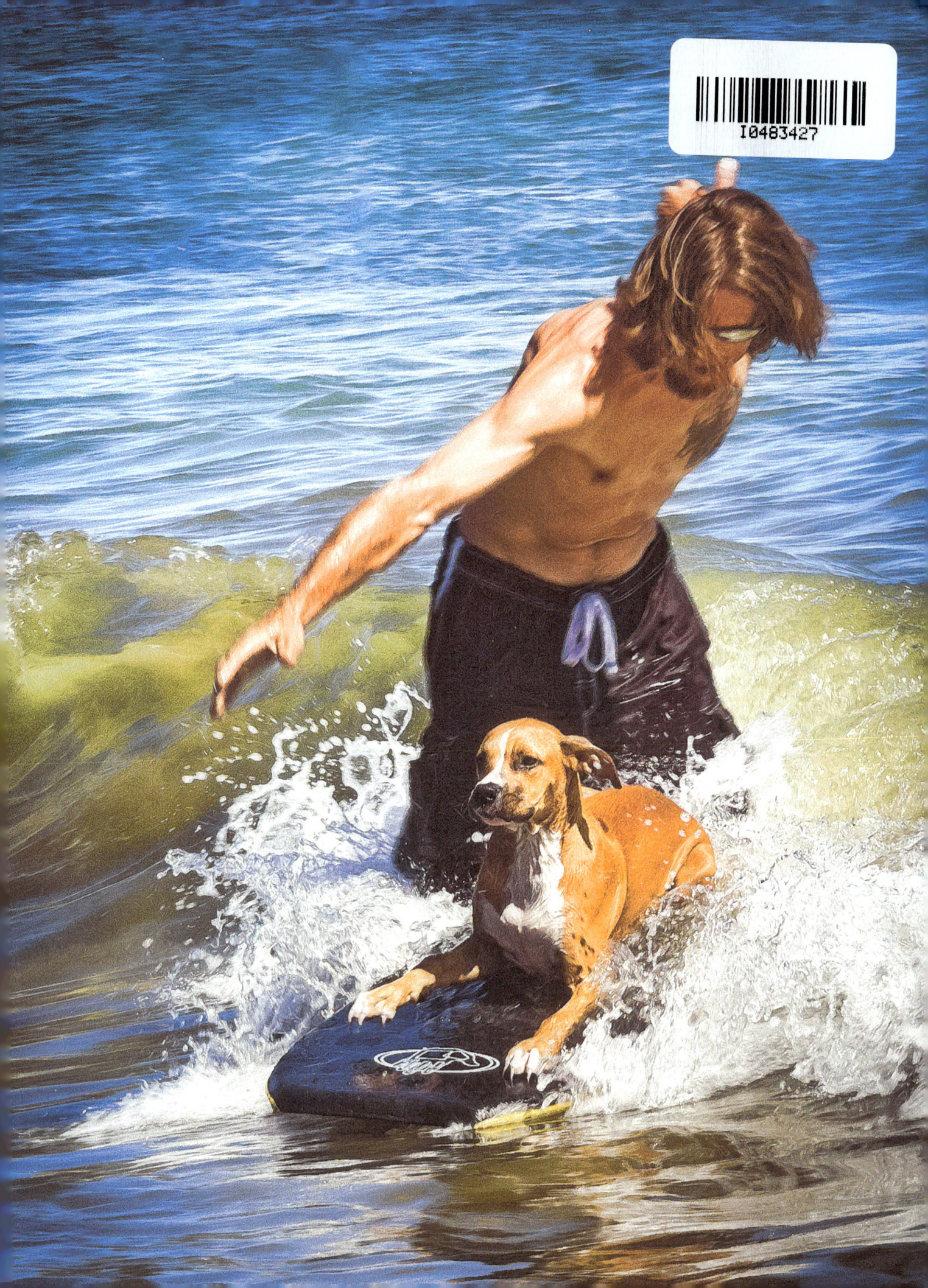

Motion Is Emotion: Action Photography Unleashed
 Published by Pathfinder Publications,
451 Lancaster St. Cambria, CA 93428.

Written by Elisabeth Haug.   http://Elisabeth Haug.com
Cover Design by Elisabeth Haug.   Interior Design by Elisabeth Haug.
First Edition ISBN (print): 978-0-9662715-9-1

If you have questions or comments about this book, or need information about licensing, custom editions, special sales, or academic/corporate purchases, please contact Elisabeth Haug, Info@EHaug.com or (760)805-8651

Other books by Elisabeth Haug:
Living Your Dream: 978-0-9662715-4-6
A Finger on the Shutter: 978-0-9662715-4-6
Dogs just want to have fun: 978-0982606407
New Age Vikings I: 978-0-9662715-5-3
New Age Vikings II: 978-0-9662715-2-2
New Age Viking III: 978-145639852
The Legend of God and Pegasus: 978-0-9662715-8-4
Eldhestar: fun, wide vision, and adventure: 978-1461094838
In the Hoofbeats of the Vikings: 978-0-9662715-0-8
California Elephant Seals: 978-0982606483
Cambria, A modern Camelot: 978-1543160611
Morro Bay: A Magical Marriage of Man Made and Nature: 978-1545566244

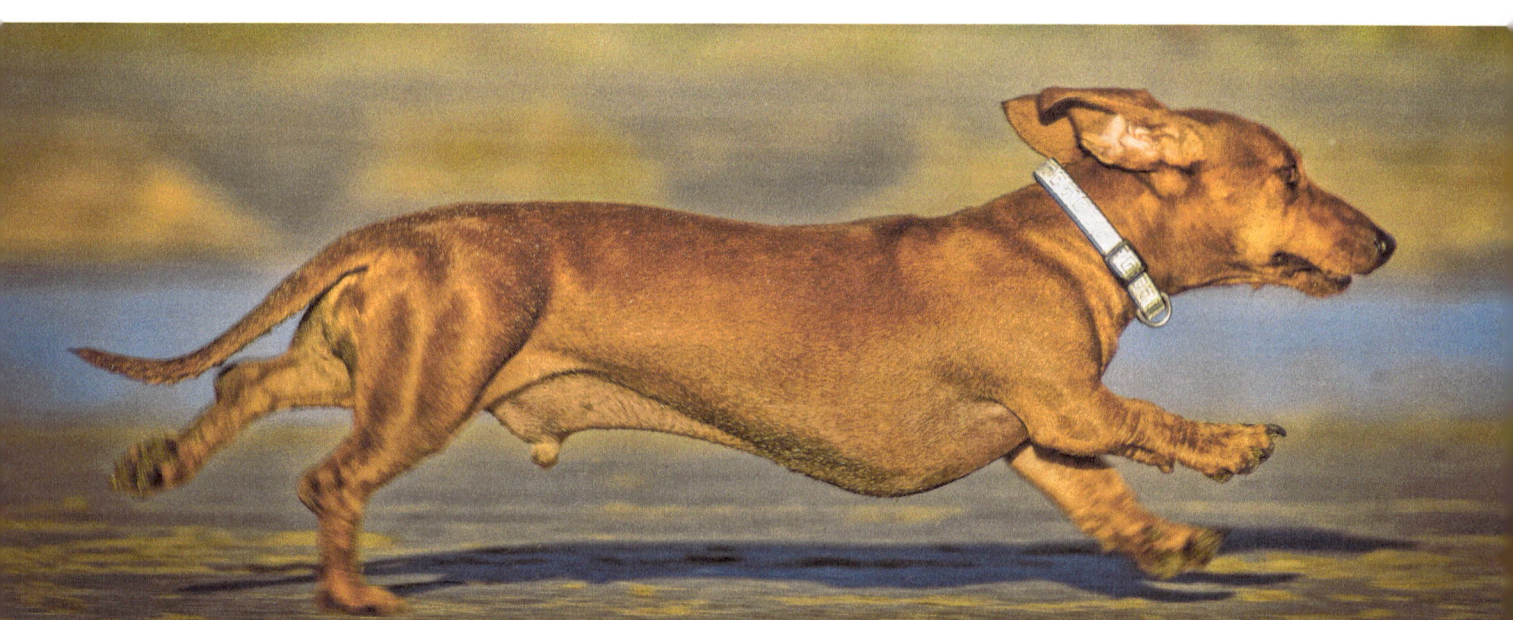

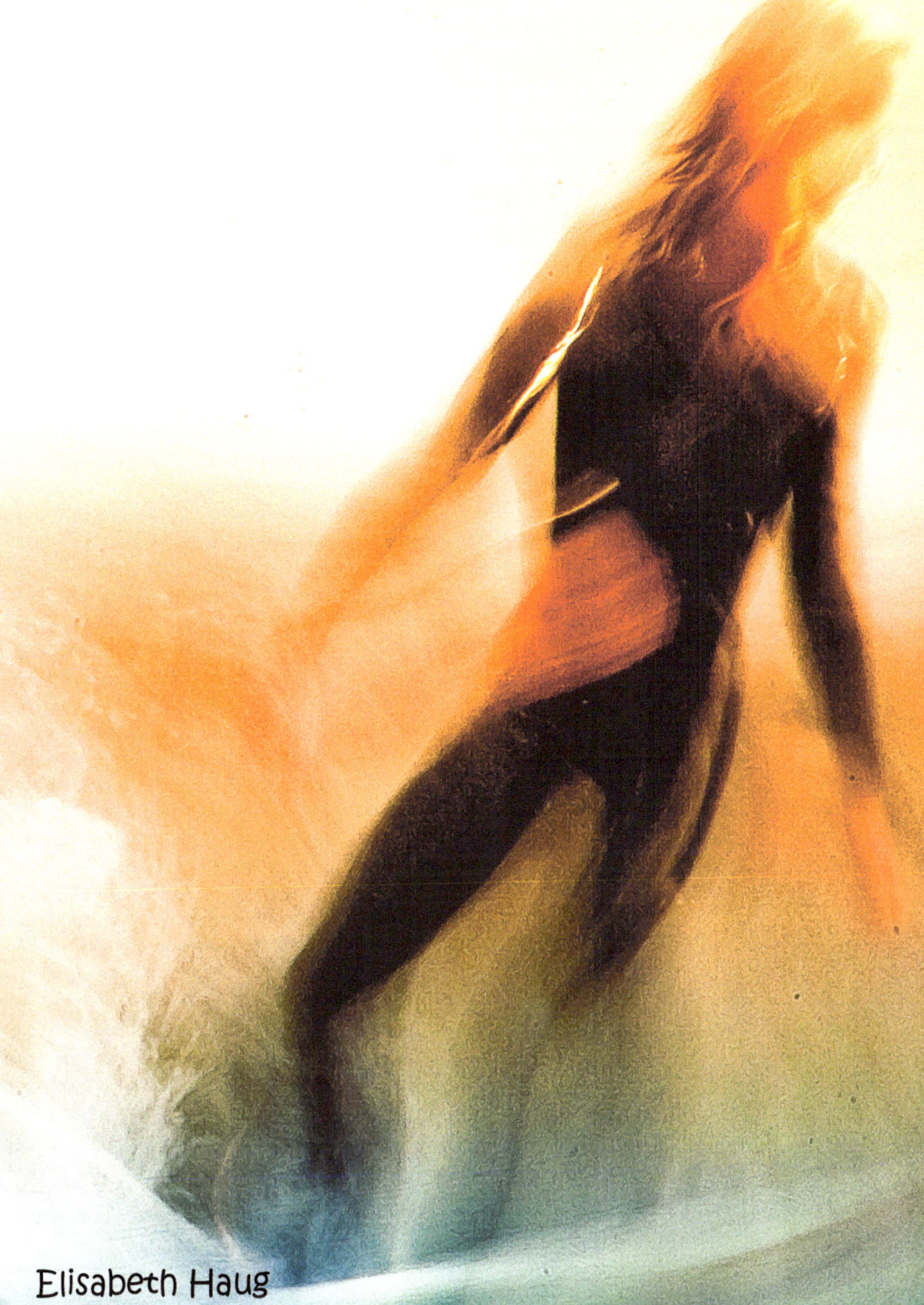

Elisabeth Haug

Motion Is Emotion
Action Photography Unleashed

There is a method to the madness in the fonts used in the book.
1. Large and bold is used for quotes. Start by reading them as you browse the photos.
2. Normal size is used for general information.
3. Italics is used for photo captions (critiques).

Why Action Photography? Photographing motion is:
- Powerful.
- Fun.
- Invigorating.
- Challenging.
- Exciting.
- Attention generating.

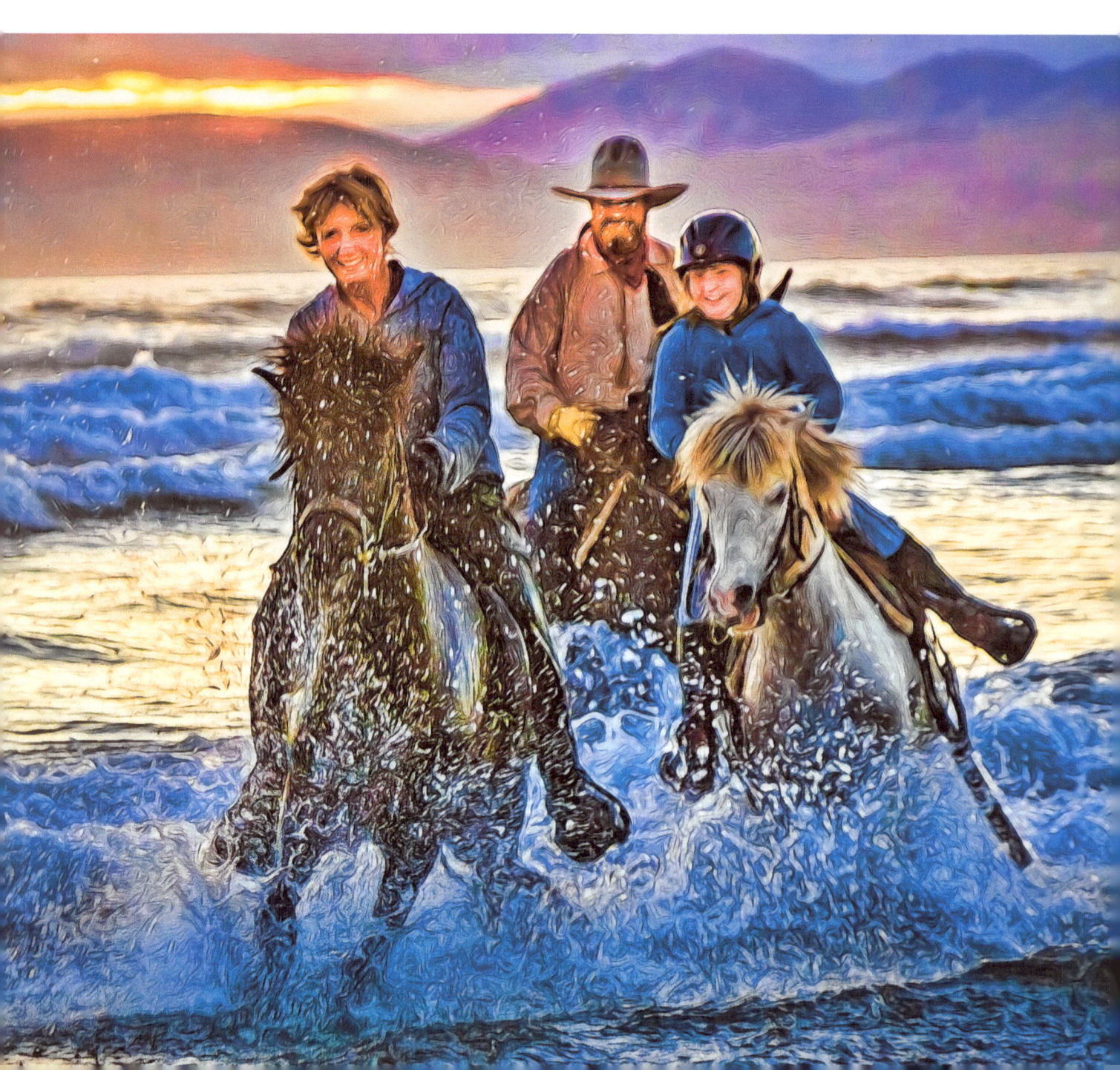

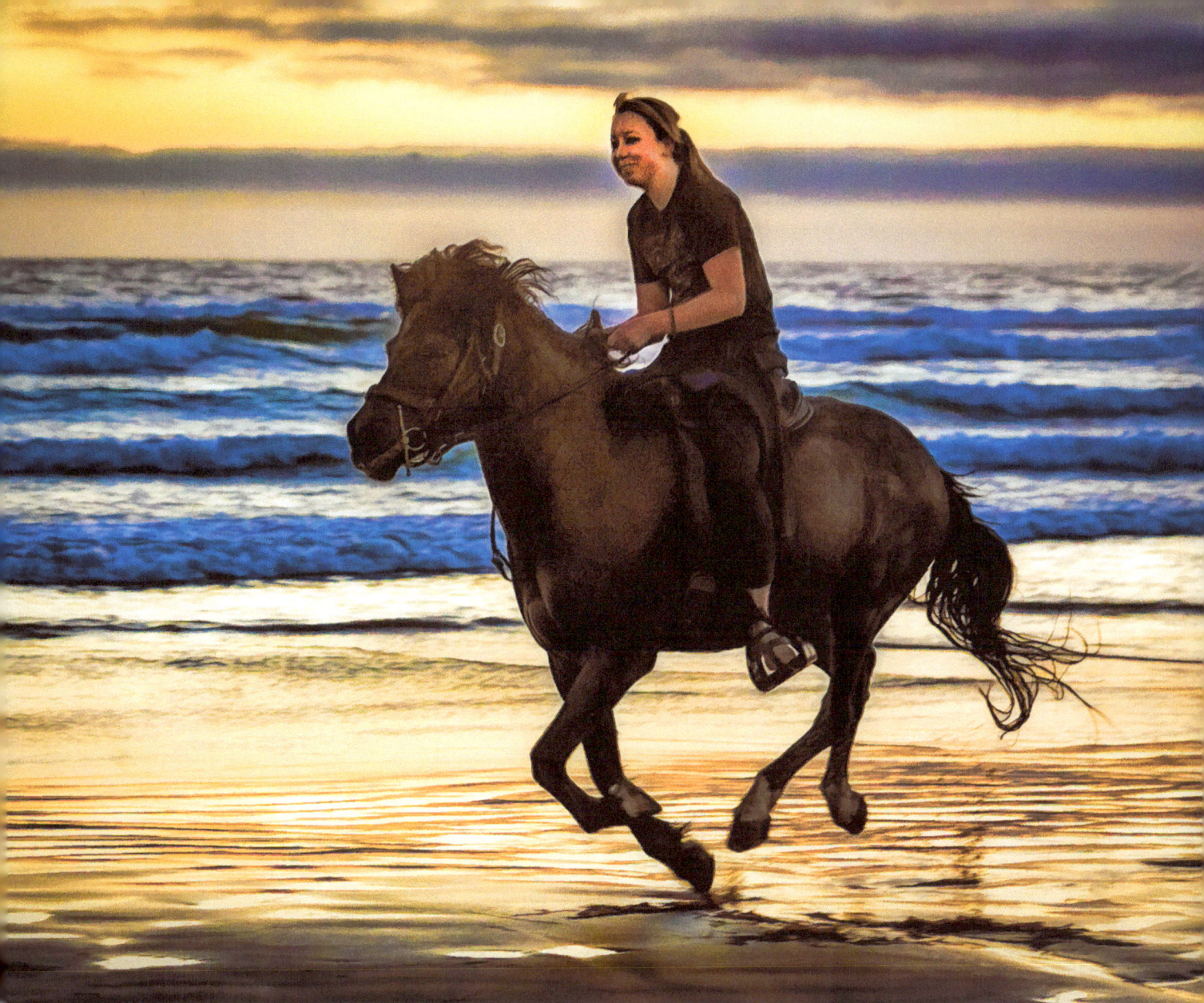

An added bonus to mastering action photography is its ability to teach you to maximize your photography in other genres as well. It improves your muscle memory and teaches you:

- To be precise.
- To be prepared.
- To be alert.
- To stay ahead of the wave and make quick decisions.
- To be trigger happy and quick on the draw.

My mission with the photos in this book is to inspire. To offer visions and ideas for photos of similar types you, too, can take and events you can set in motion.

The images on this and the following spread are from an outing with friends on Pismo Beach in Central California. It took place many years ago when digital cameras were not as capable as they are today. But I still smile when I view the results. Needless to say, we had fun. What events with friends can you set in motion?

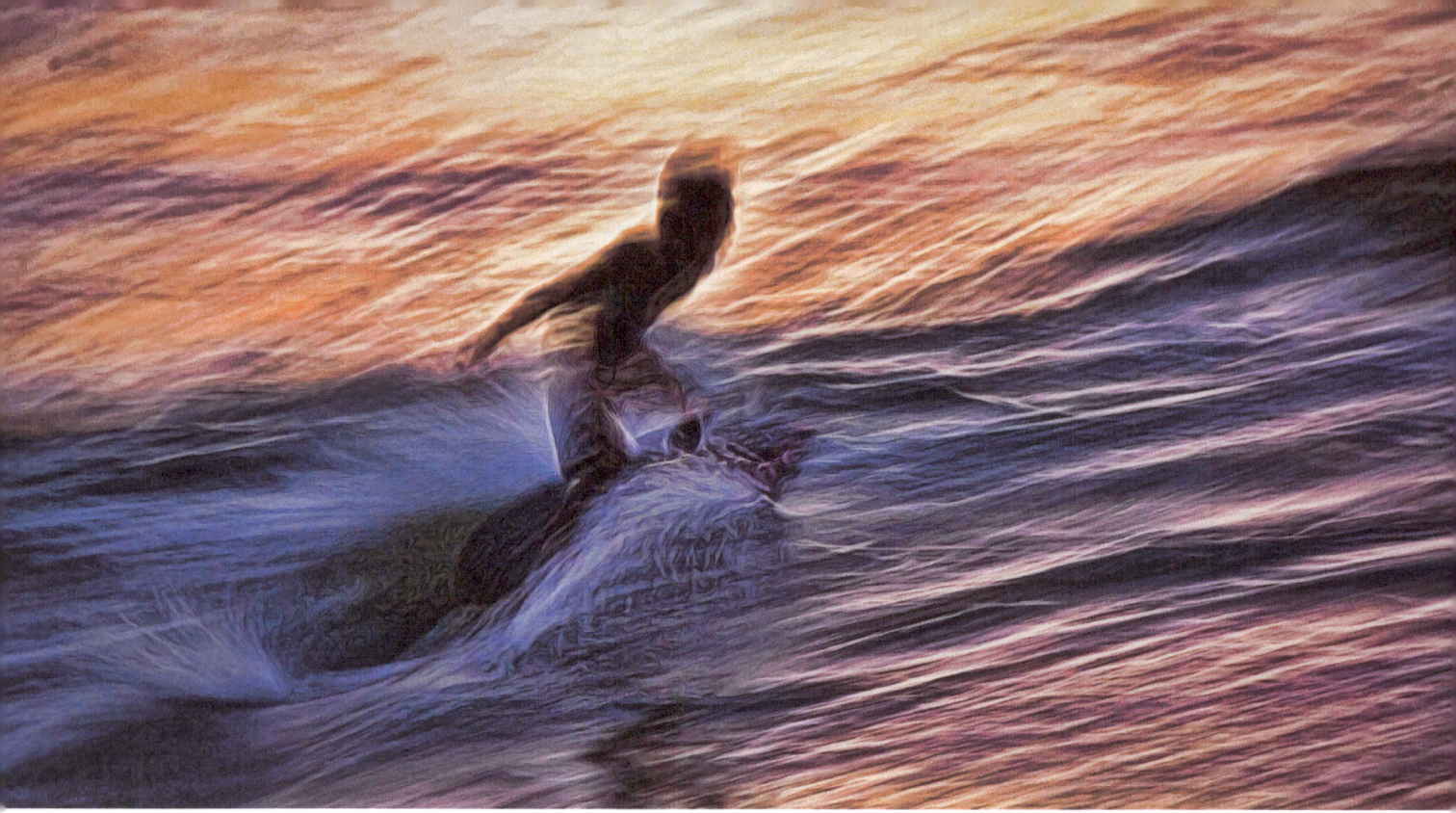

What is action photography?

To make sure I had my facts straight, I Googled "action photography" when I first thought of creating this book. I randomly chose two dictionary sites from a suggested list.
- *Collins*: A still photograph that shows someone or something in motion
- *Dictionary.com :* A photographic picture featuring the subject in motion or action; also called action picture, action shot.

We tend to associate action photography with high speed motion, but notice speed is not mentioned in either of the dictionaries' definitions. That means even images with very slow action speeds are considered action shots.

What makes that especially interesting is that the techniques for photographing fast and slow motion are basically identical. You have to be a tad more *on the ball* when the action is fast, of course. But otherwise, the process is the same.

In fact, most successful strategies for action photography work equally well with other genres. Nothing remains the same for very long. Light changes; sitting birds take off; grazing wild life flee; sitting children erupt into action; and facial expressions change.

Maximize your results by thinking like a lawman from the old West. Be aware, alert, prepared, and fast on the draw. Shoot from the hip!

Flow is crucial.

Everything has a flow—traffic, water, stories, music, movies, photos, motion, light, blood, thoughts, and ideas. Some flows engage more than others. And some are more harmonious. Some feel pleasant and some are disruptive.

Creating an interesting, uninterrupted flow in your images is paramount. Lead your viewer's eye easily from the point of interest (main subject} in the photo along an imaginary cookie crumb trail through all the other pertinent points of your story.

Flow is especially important in action photography. All motion has a pattern whether it be the footfall of animals, the way a surfer catches the waves and rides them, or the way cars and bicycles follow roads.

All motion has peaks and valleys. Peaks are when the impulsion is greatest and the motion is at its most powerful. Whenever possible photograph motion right before its peak or exactly at it. Once the peak has passed, so has the momentum. Then the viewer's interest immediately wanes.

Photographing galloping horses with all four feet off the ground (as in the photo below) **can** *be an exciting motif* **but only** *while the horse is in the upward phase of the leap.*

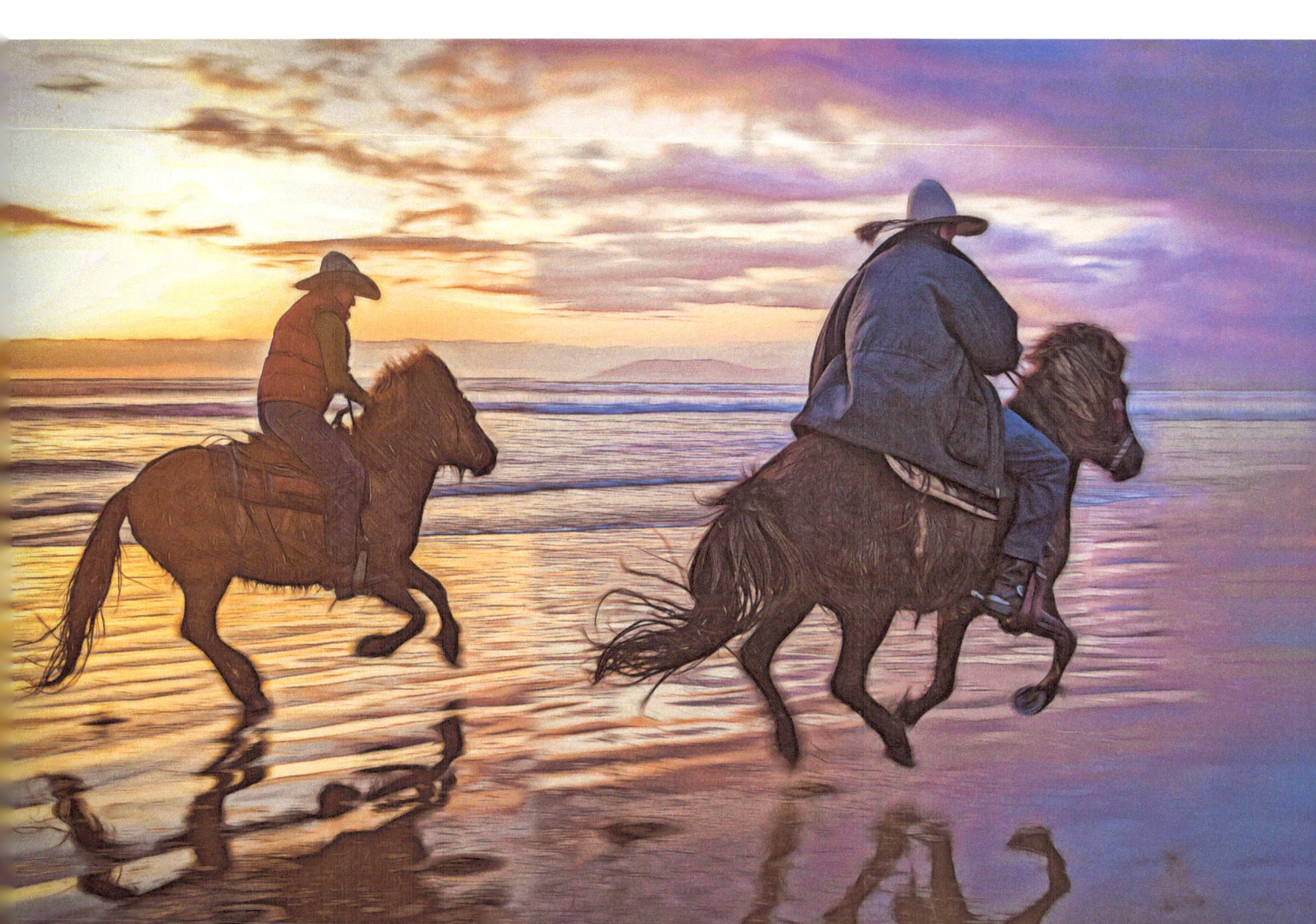

Remember fun is the best antidote for burnout!

Photography is the language of emotion. It is understood by everyone regardless of cultural barriers. Use it to share your feelings, your point of view, your voice, and your vision.

In photography (and life) you get what you focus on. Choose to focus on what you want more of in your life rather than what you fear.

Great photography has two components: art and craft. Craft is the sum of you equipment and your skill in using it. Art is the part of yourself you invest in the endeavor.

Except being a tad more extreme, the secrets of action photography are the same as those of all other photo genres.

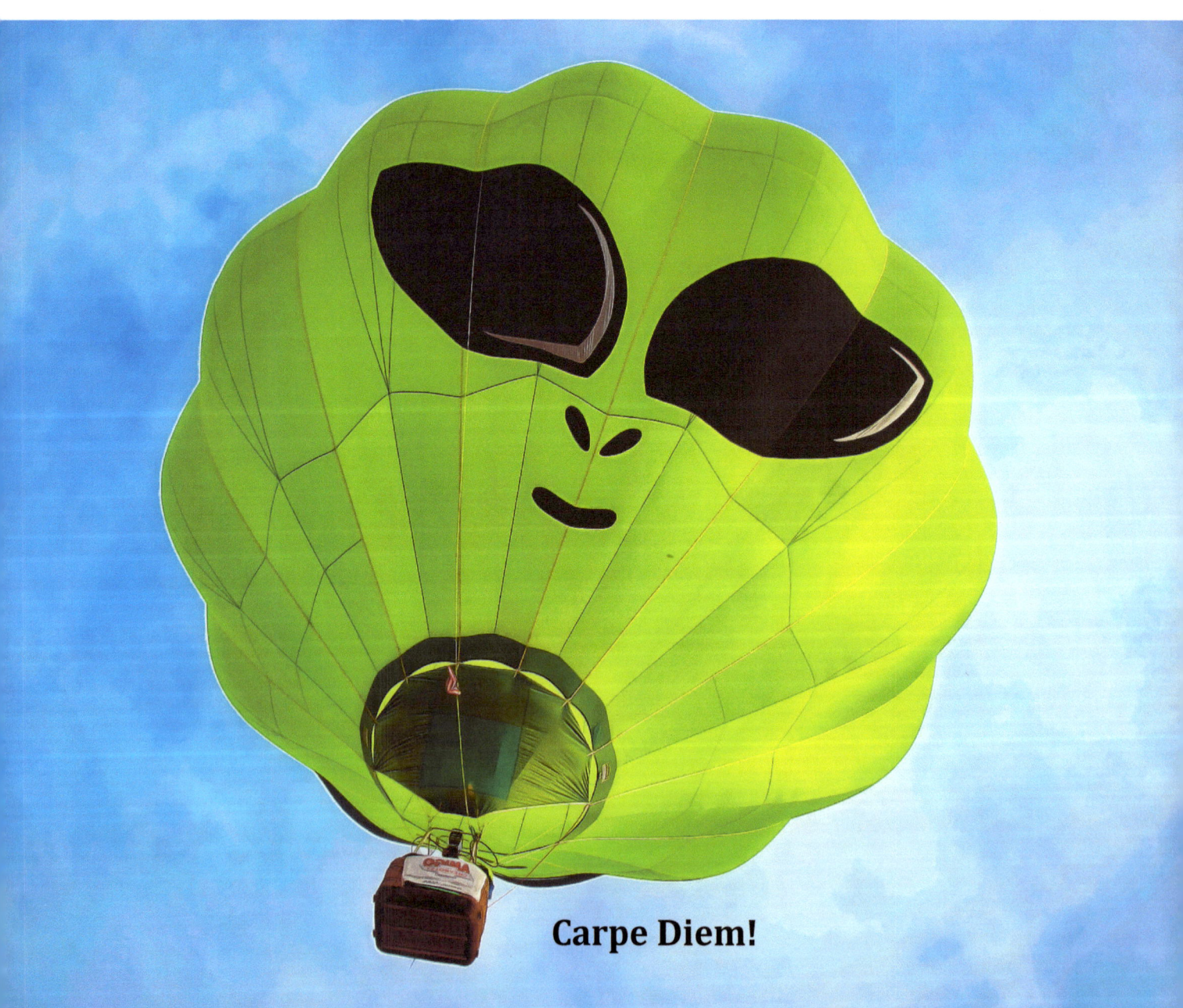

Carpe Diem!

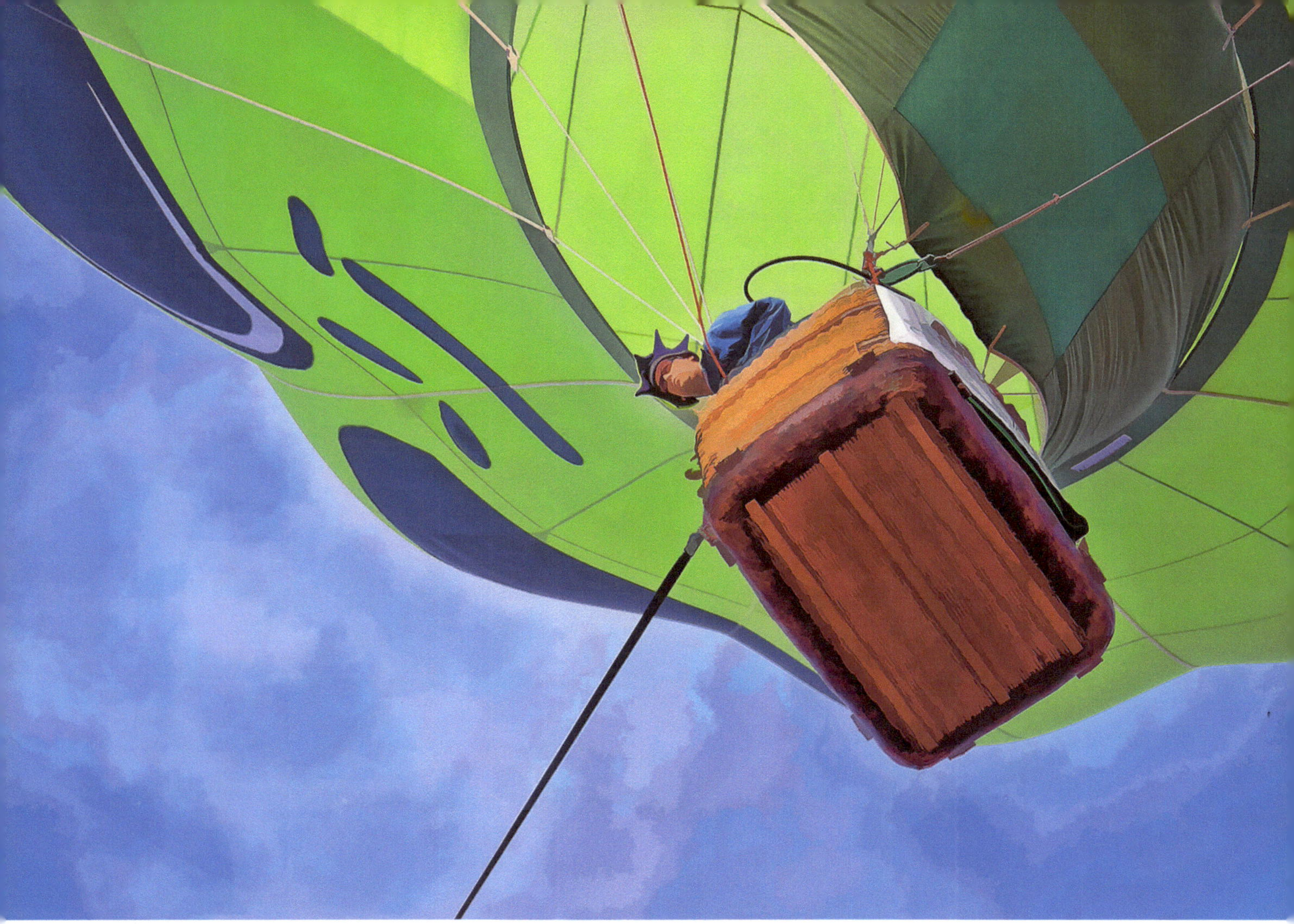

Everyone loves balloons! Consider attending a balloon festival.

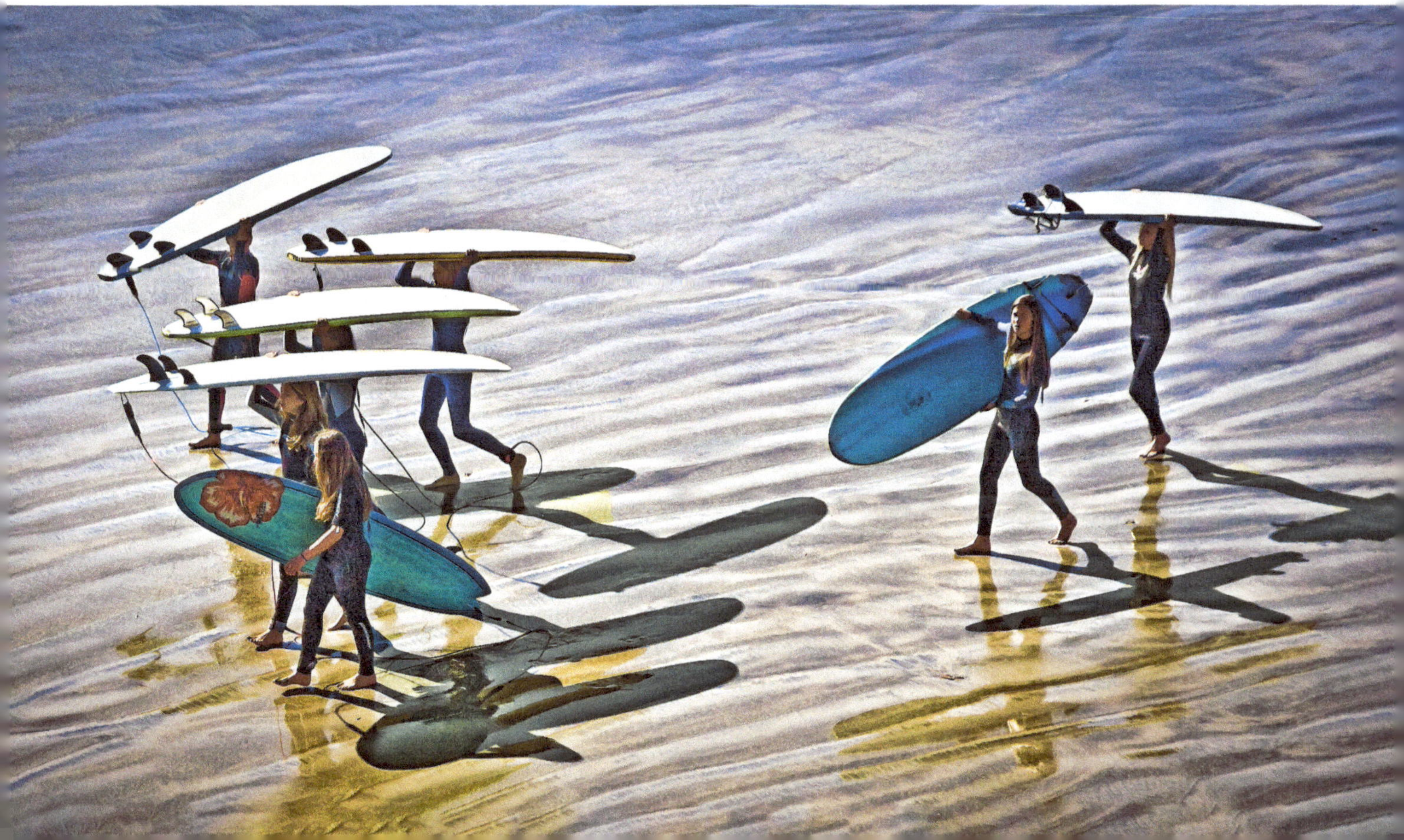

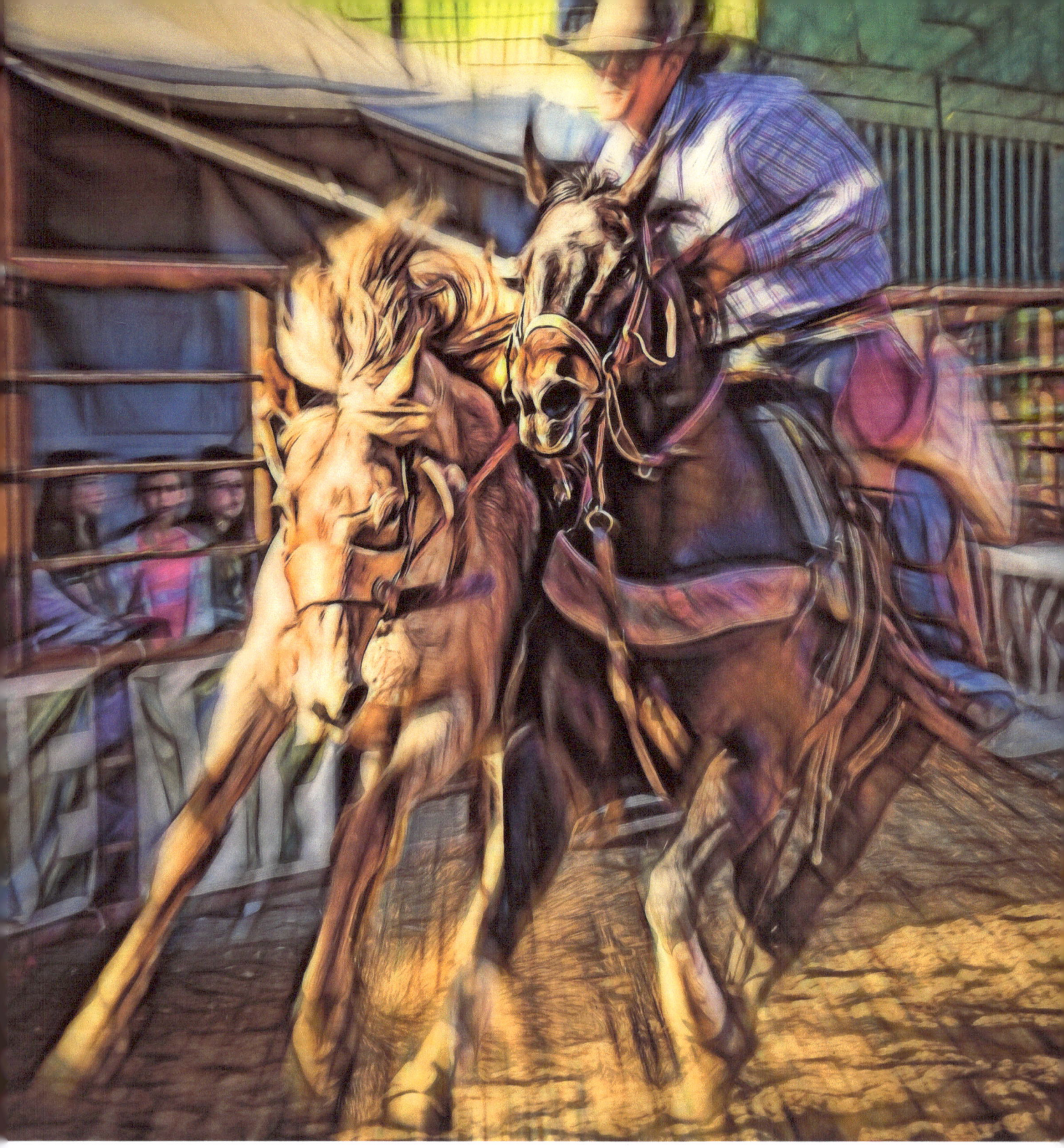

The Central California Coast where I live has a wealth of exciting events. The local rodeo above and wind surfing to the right are a few. Check out exciting events in your neighborhood!

The photo above is an example of zoom blur. Ideally zoom blur photos will —like this one— have a clear focus (the brown horse's head). The photo to the right has frozen action. The windsurfers and the waves are all moving.

How Do You Shoot Action?

The four most common methods are:
- Freeze the action—fast shutter speed.
- Random blur—slow shutter speed with no distinct focus.
- Panning—slow shutter speed with parallel camera pacing action.
- Zoom Blur—slow shutter speed while holding the camera still facing the subject as it moves towards you. Some photographers use zooming at slow shutter speeds to get the same effect.

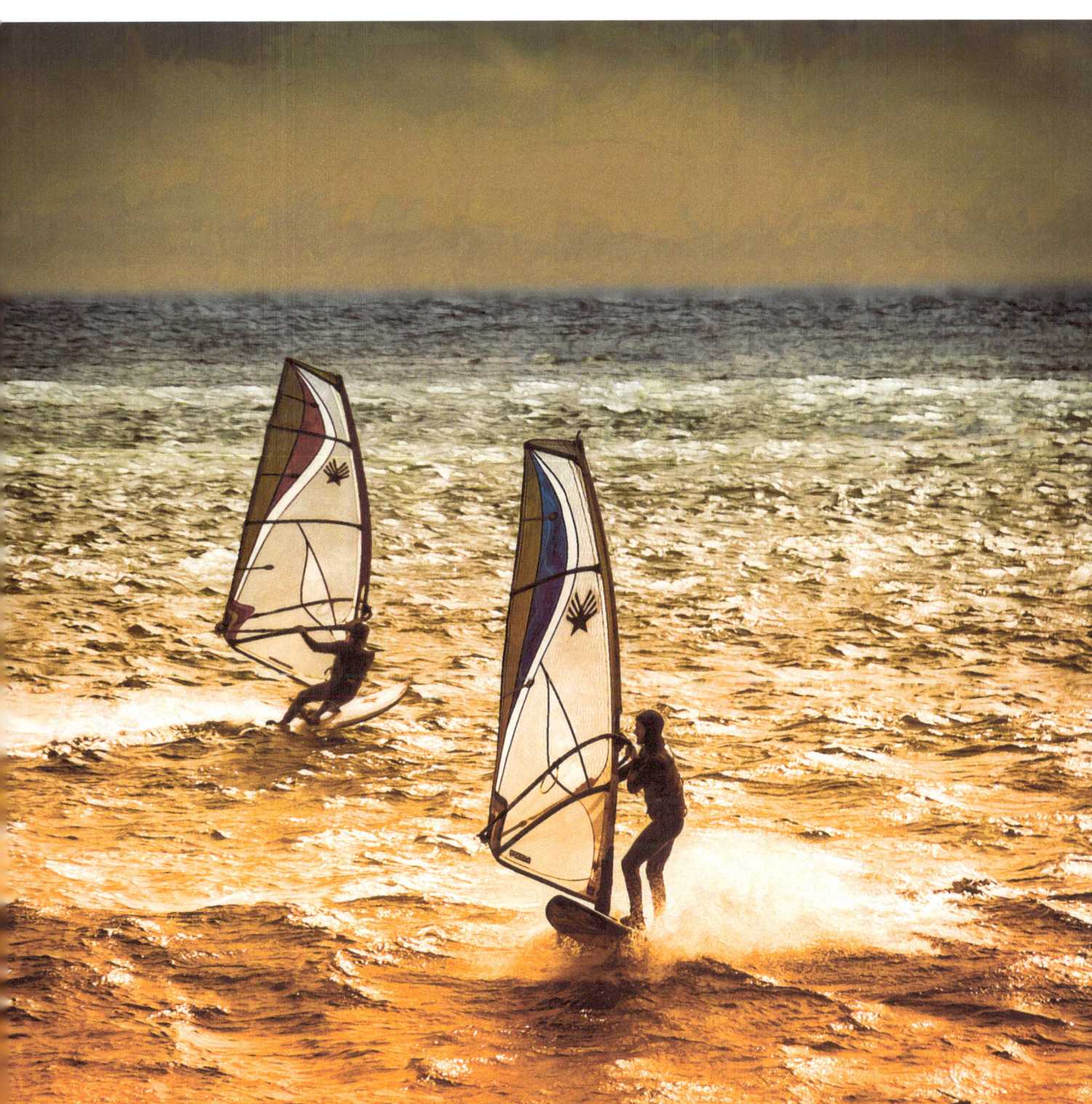

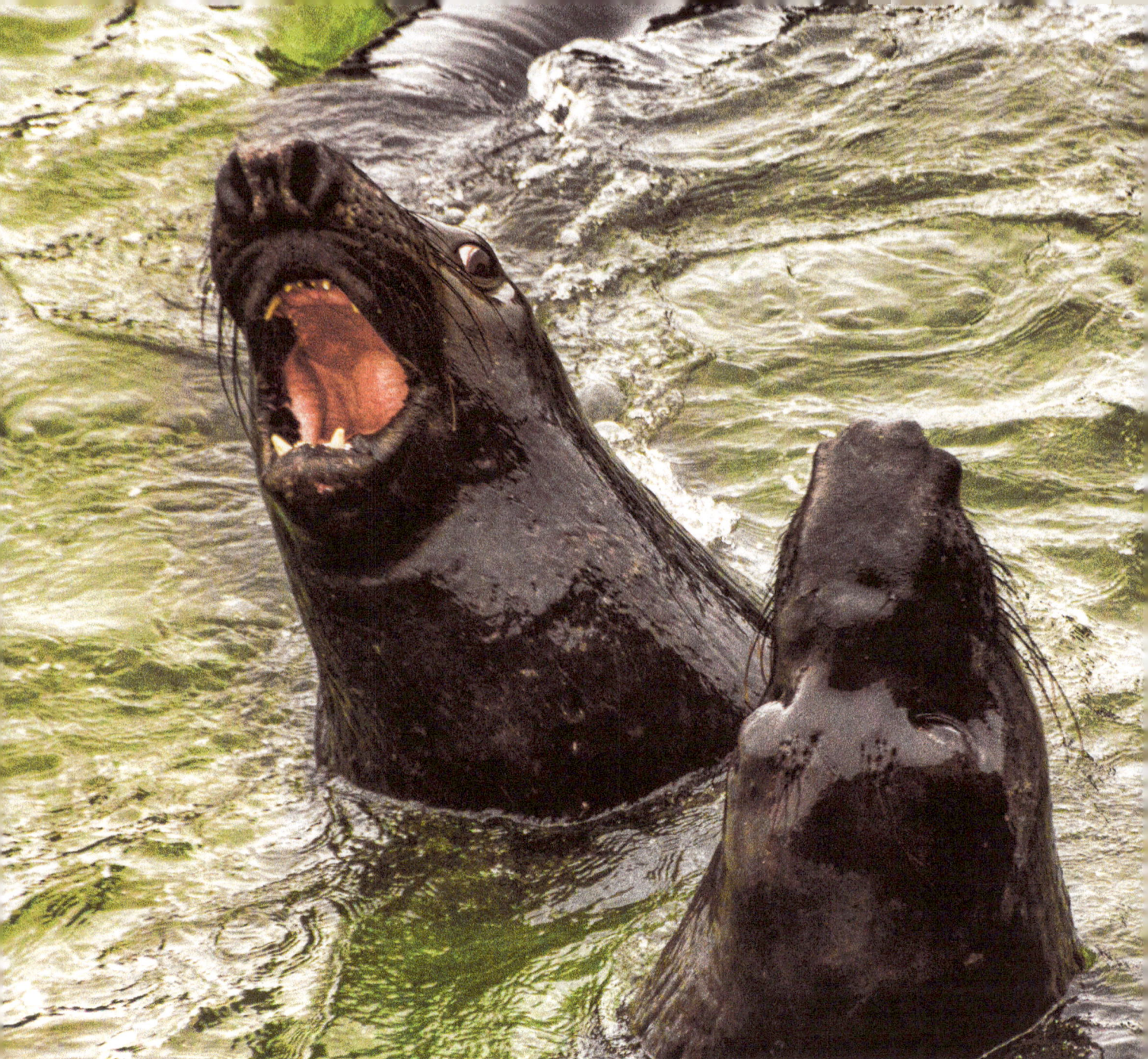

Choose shutter speed priority mode in your settings when shooting action.

The Elephant Seals in the photos on this spread are humongous. The adult males weigh 5000 pounds. Adult males love to spar and have elephant like noses. They make funny noises and are so ugly that they are cute.

They spend most of their life in the ocean, coming ashore for a month just twice a year. The northern variety only beach close to where I live in Central California.

Are there any interesting sights, activities, and/or wild life in your neighborhood you haven't photographed, yet?

The most common—and generally the most productive—way of shooting action is to "freeze it" causing the motion to be tack sharp. An extremely fast shutter speed locks the subject's position during the exposure.

When freezing action, use a shutter speed of 1/1000 of a second for fast moving subjects and long lenses. If you are shooting wider angle and slower speeds you can safely choose a somewhat slower shutter speed, especially if your camera and/or lens has some type of image stabilization.

Rule of thumb:
- Because of camera shake, the more zoom (longer lens) used, the faster the required shutter speed.
- The faster and the more complicated the action is, the higher the required shutter speed.
- Given the same ISO, higher shutter speeds leads to a wider aperture (larger lens opening) and give less depth of field. Most often, this is an advantage when you are selectively focusing on your subject because it is usual to want the point of interest to stand out from the background.

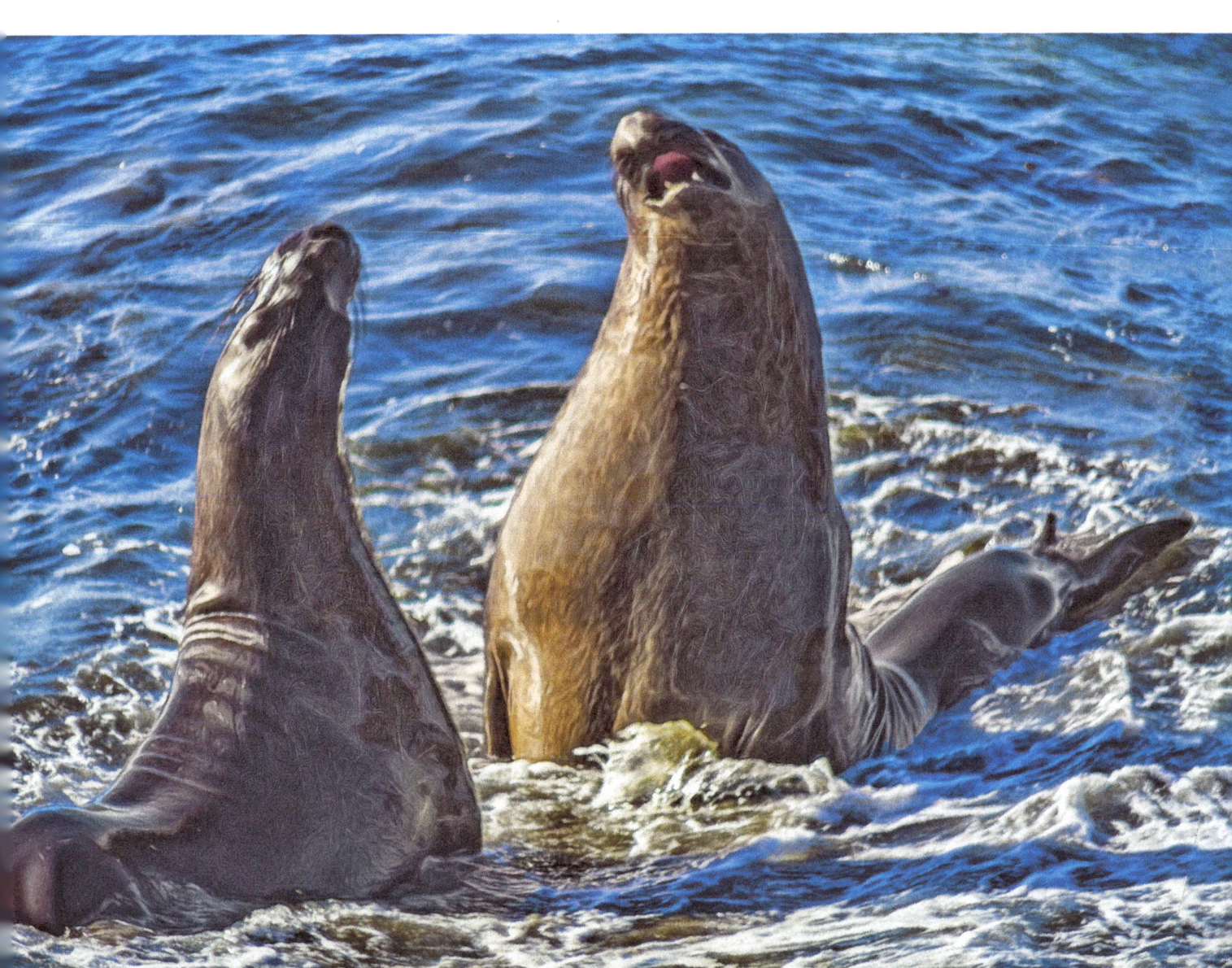

Any shot worth taking, is worth taking in raw. Take a companion jpeg (by adjusting your settings) if you need a quick fix. But don't limit your later options by neglecting to save a raw file, too.

Understanding the basics of how digital photography works is important when maximizing your photography.

Whereas film photography is a chemical process, digital images result from the creation of computer files. Information about the subject and its surroundings are recorded at the time of the shoot and then—after the fact—saved in one or more file formats (photo for jpeg and a data type for raw).

When shooting film, an exposure leads to a negative—one uninterrupted picture surface, Digital exposure files are mosaics composed of a high number of minute pixels. Each pixel contains all the pertinent information about the tiny area of the picture it covers—color, saturation, light, sharpness, etc. Matters are simplified by dividing the pixels into groups—a.k.a clusters.

Check out the photo on the right hand page to view the principle. The tiles are only meant to demonstrate the concept and are many times bigger than actual individual clusters. (The effect has been created using the distort filter in Photoshop.)

For most, water is not the first thing that comes to mind as an action photography subject. Yet, water is not only beautiful but one of the most powerful forces of all—both when seen alone and when something or someone is in it. Do you live close to the ocean or do you have a lake, a river, or a stream nearby?

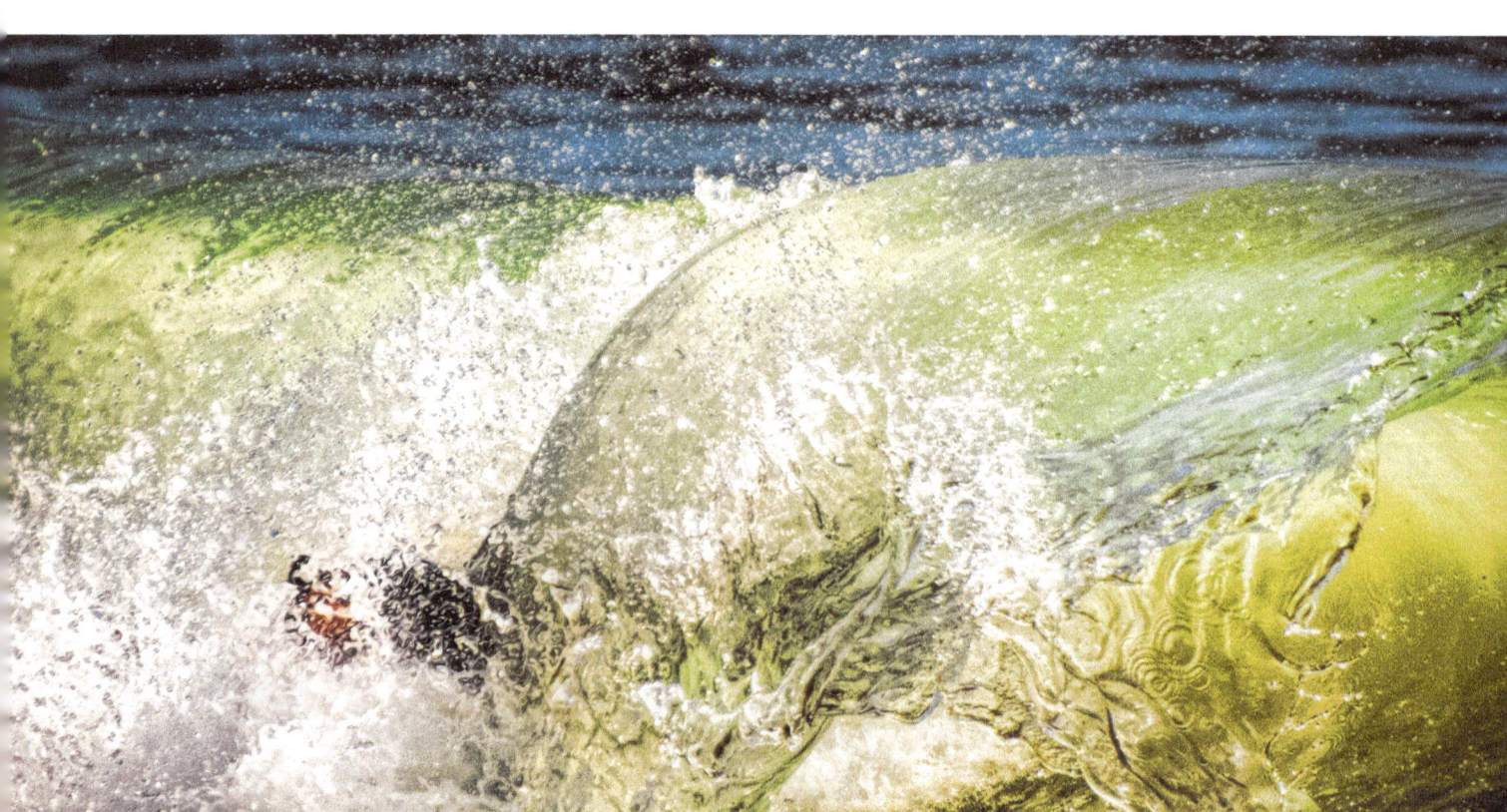

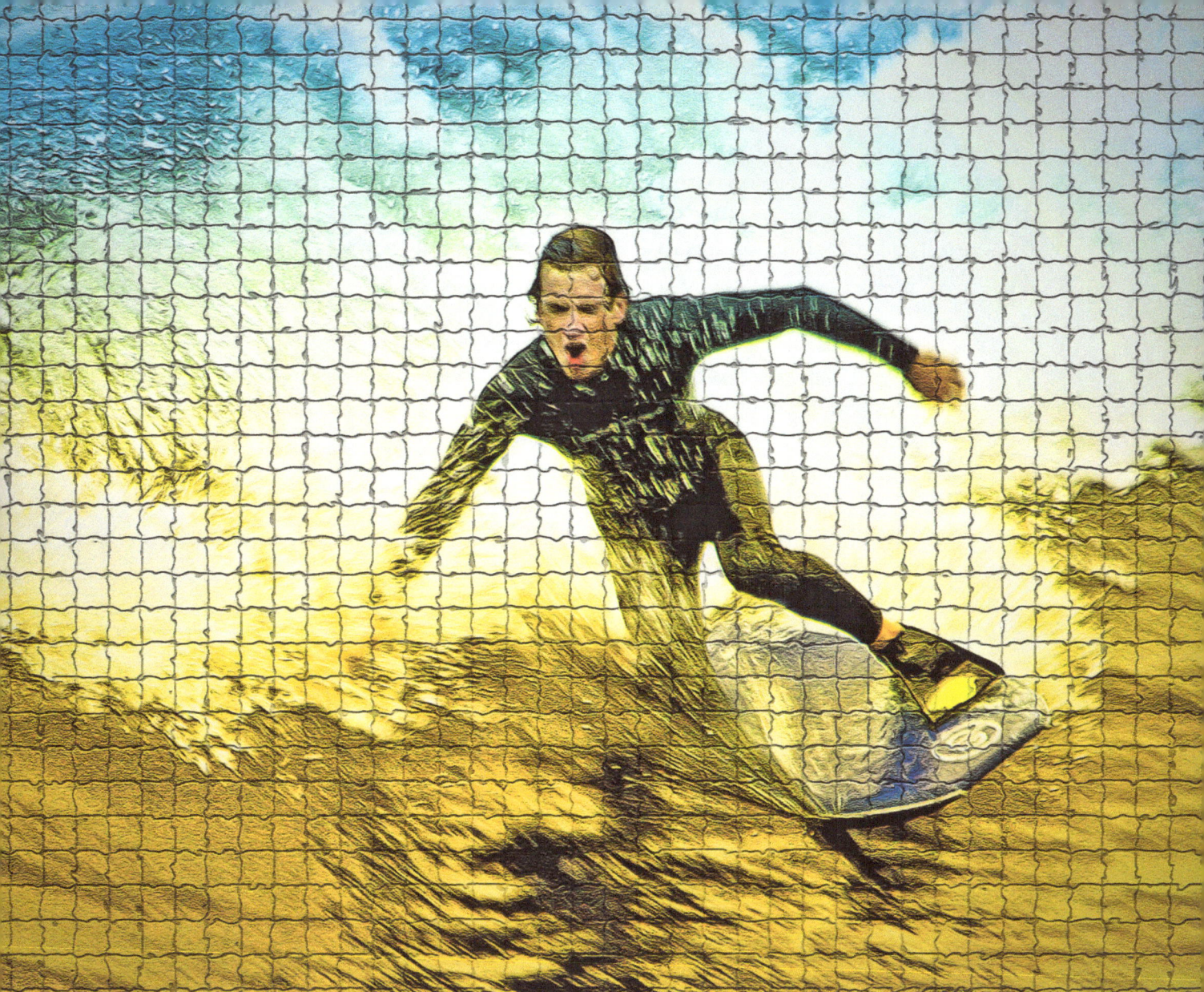

Higher end modern cameras allow you to choose between the two ways of saving the gleaned pixel information into files—jpeg and raw.

In jpeg, the information is converted into a photo file (a finished image) immediately after you click. Apart from the settings you can decide on before shooting—such as file size, white balance, exposure compensation, and picture style—the photographer leaves it up to the camera to make all the software decisions. Furthermore, in order to optimize its size, the file is compressed during the saving. This results is degradation of image quality.

Nowadays, the jpeg compression damage is not nearly as serious as it used to be. Nonetheless, the process is harmful. Also, every time you later save any jpeg, it deteriorates even further. This is true even when no changes have been made to the file. The decline is the result of the new compression. **Therefore, always save your processed files—even jpegs— as tiffs or Photoshop files.**

When shooting in raw, the camera leaves the file interpretation up to the photographer. It records the information as a data type file. There is no compression. Through the use of a raw plug, the photographer can change whatever information he wants in the data file without repercussions. Once he is satisfied with his result, he can save it in uncompressed file formats like tiff and Photoshop as well as in jpeg.

Today, practically all editing software—even the free ones—have a raw file converter. The photographer has numerous choices of adding his own touch by changing the stored information non-destructively. For example, rather than accept the camera's choice of exposure, the photographer can choose his own preferences anywhere in a range of three stops.

In many cases the photographer can make similar changes to his jpegs in an editing program. But the cost of doing so is image quality degradation.

The advantages to shooting in raw are higher quality image files and considerably more control for the photographer. The downsides to raw are the step added to the work flow and the added file size. Hard drives and picture cards are becoming less and less costly, making file size a small concern compared to what it used to be.

The bane of digital photography is noise. It occurs when the transition between pixel clusters isn't as smooth as it should be. The result is a number stray pixels of inconsistent color and/or luminance.

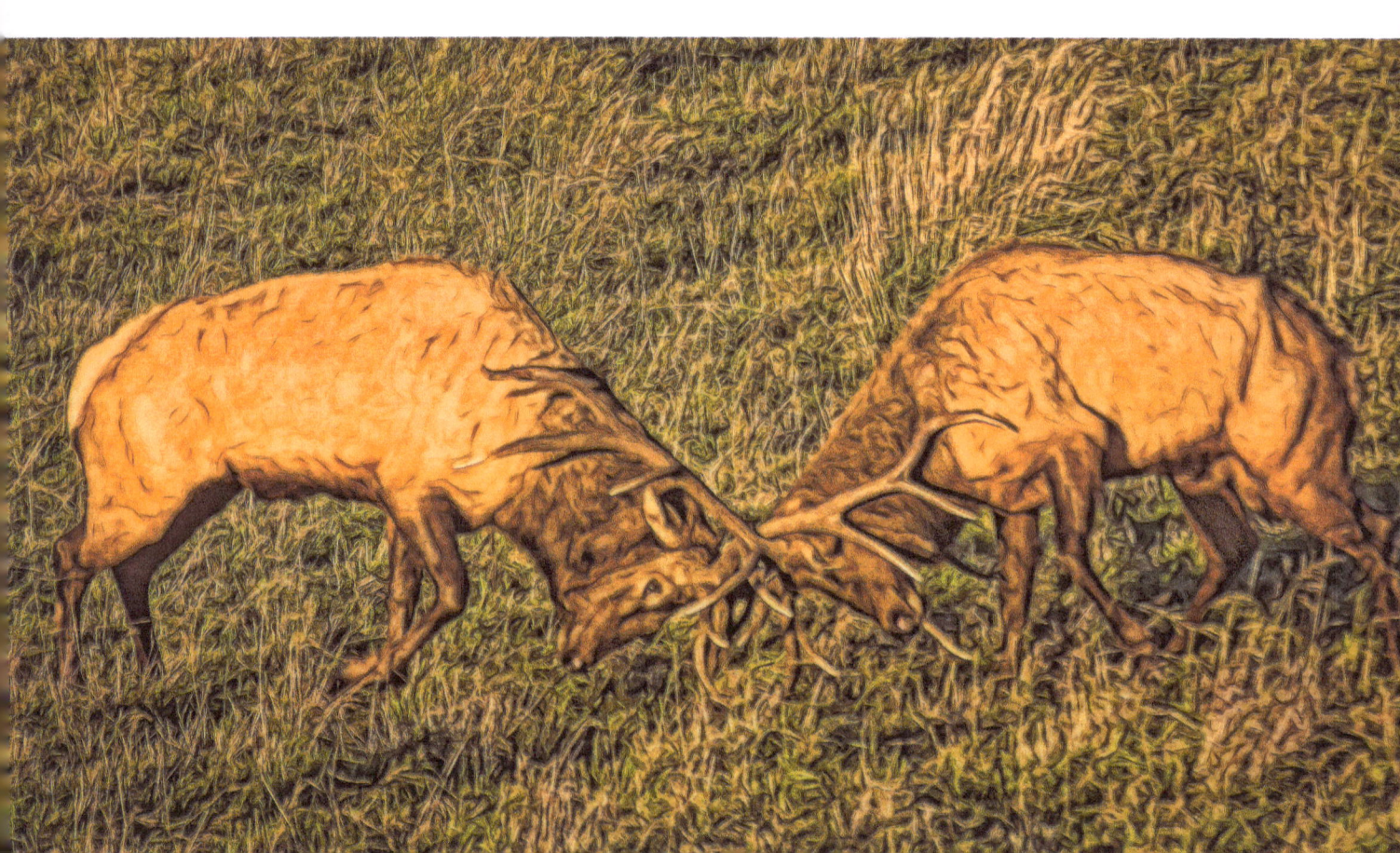

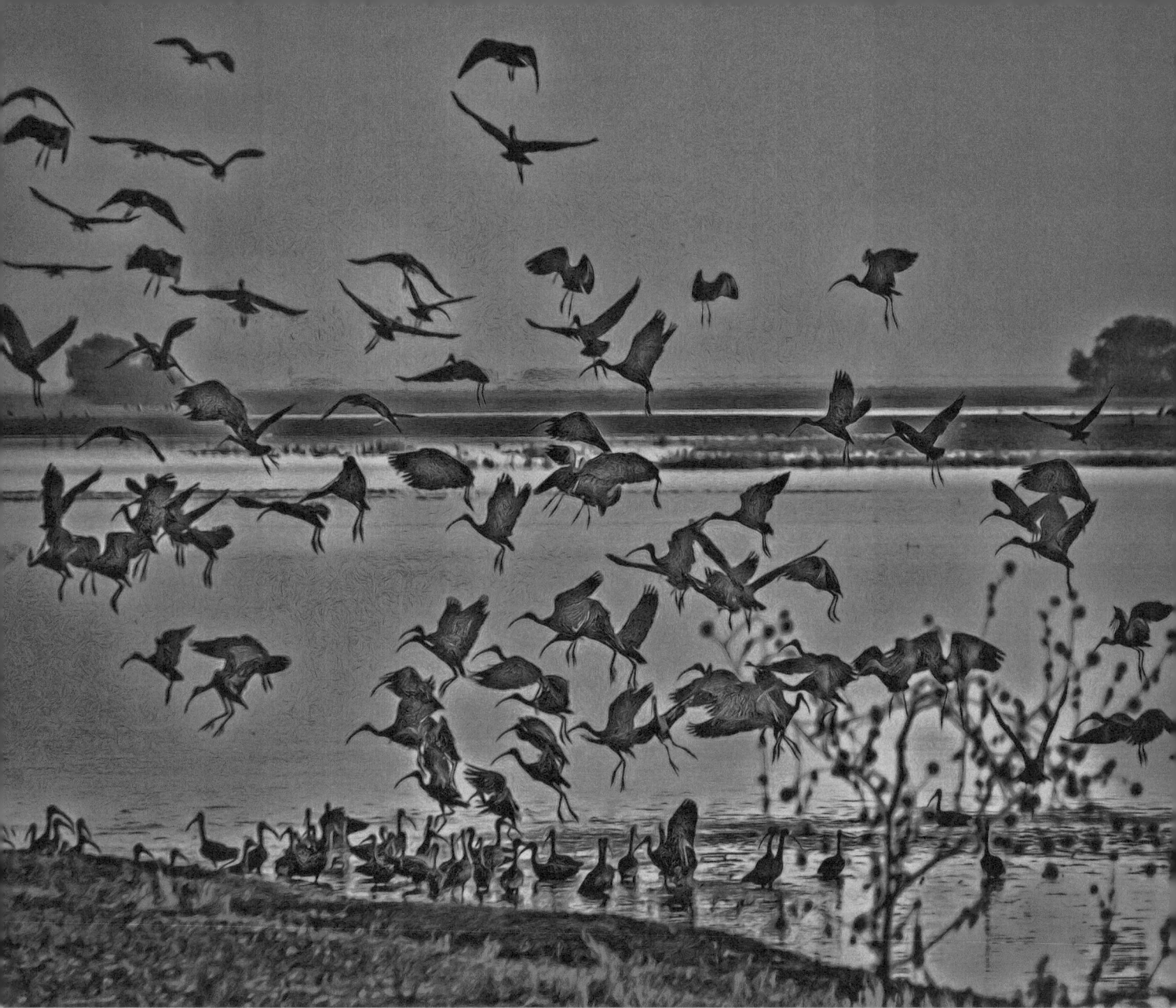

Noise is considered unprofessional and is distracting and unsightly. It is most common at high ISO and in jpegs. It is more dominant in dark, shadowy areas. Now a days—using later model cameras and updated image reduction software—excessive noise is no longer as destructive as it used to be. Nonetheless, noise is something to be constantly on the alert for—especially in fast shutter speed situations in low light settings.

One of my personal favorite camera advances is auto ISO. Auto ISO will choose the lowest workable ISO in any given situation. Additionally, it can help you make more educated choices as to whether to go ahead with your exposure as planned or to make changes. Simply keep an eye on the—by the camera suggested—ISO numbers and decide whether they are too high for you or not.

Expect the unexpected and be prepared to seize opportunities!

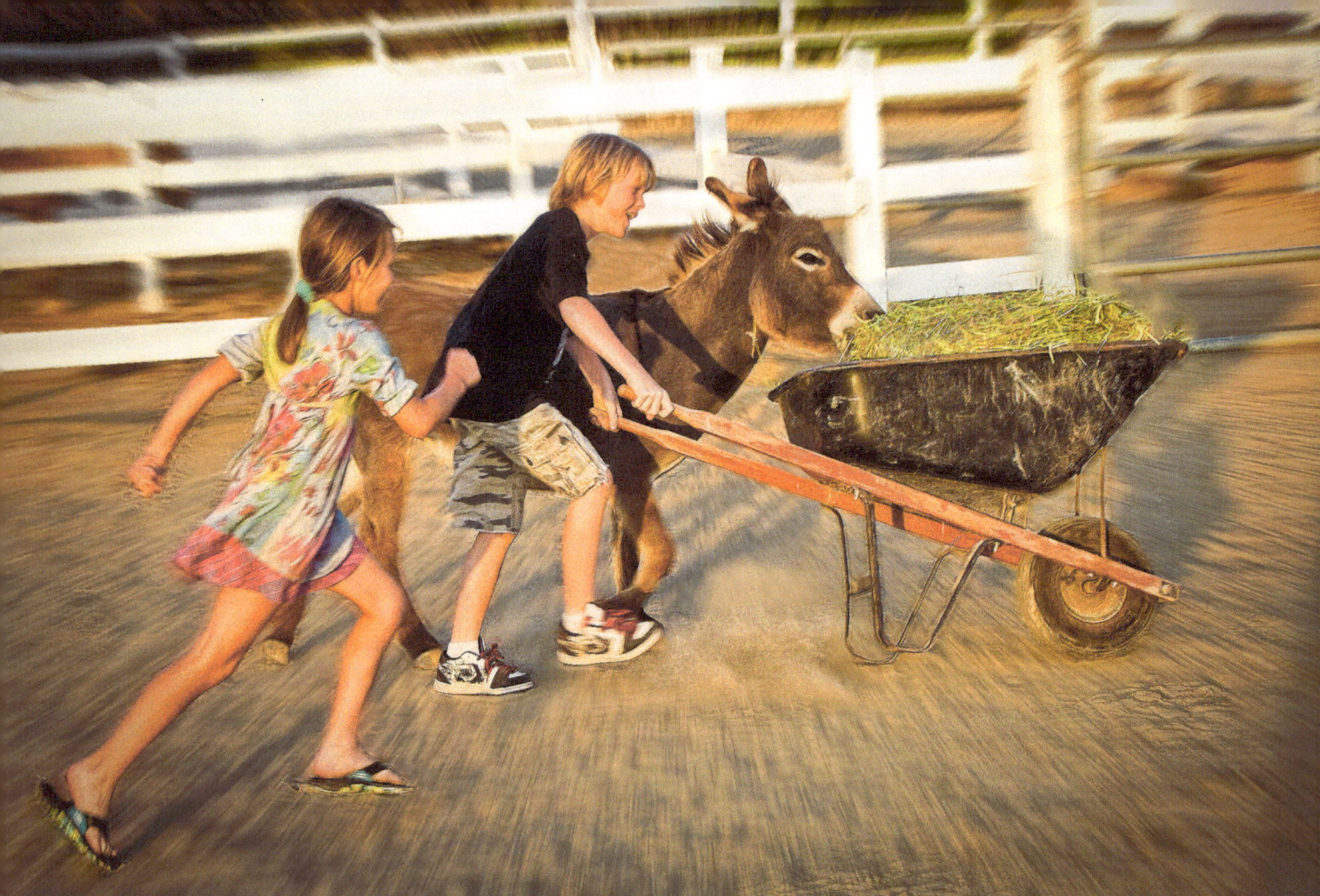

Try something new every day! Embrace failure. Realize it is a prerequisite for success!

All is not necessarily lost if your action freeze shot is not as sharp as you would like it to be. If it appeals to you in other ways, just call it a slow speed blur.

What more than sharpness needs to fall in place when shooting action photography?
- Attractive exposure.
- An interesting subject.
- A unique point of view.
- A strong connection to the viewer.
- A strong, pleasing composition with a clear point of interest (clear focus on main character) and strong leading lines.
- A powerful, engaging story.
- An uncluttered background without disturbing distractions.
- Motion caught at peak or just before it!
- Attractive light.

With only a split second to get this long list of "ducks in a rows" at the time of the shot, it is no wonder many photographers are disappointed and give up on action photography after just a few less than satisfactory attempts.

Life is great. The more you embrace fun and joy, the more you will receive.

Both of the photos on this spread are taken in the San Diego, California area—the one to the left at a friend's ranch and the one below on the beach. Both have an inviting, energetic theme of love of life, fun, and joy. Notice the synchronicity in the subjects' body positions.

Both photos were shot as action freezes. But because of the distracting back- ground in the one on the left hand page, I created a bit of zoom blur in the computer making my subjects (point of interest) stand out more. The effect also accentuates the not so fast, but energetic action.

Notice the tiny person in the top left hand of the picture below. In your opinion does it add or detract from the photo?

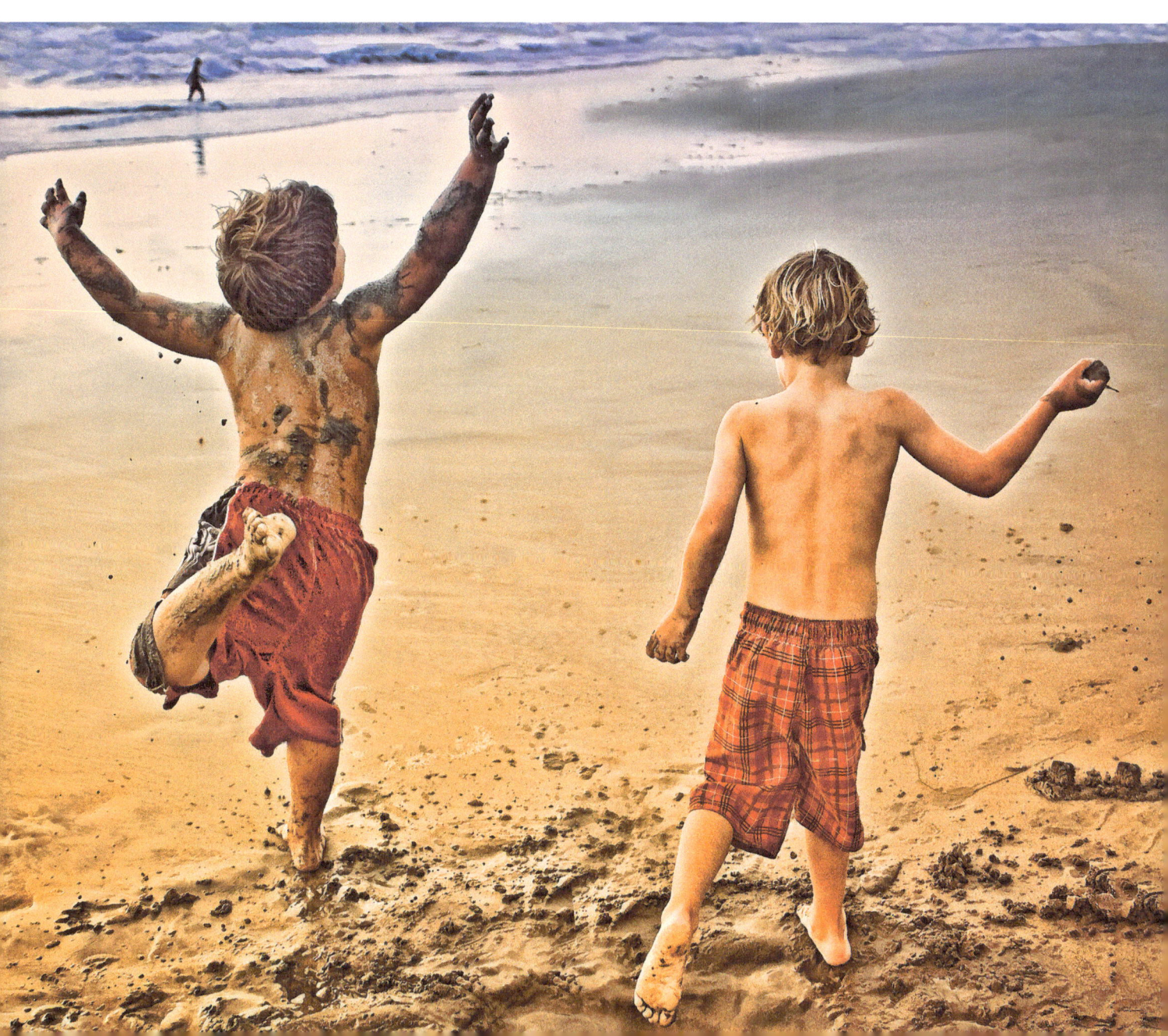

With so many other interesting and rewarding genres, is action photography really worth the effort? My answer is a resounding yes! It is true that photographing action is challenging, but it is also fun, invigorating, energizing, and enlightening.

Furthermore, no other type of photography gets the instant attention that action shots do. If you place two photos in front of a viewer—one with motion and one without—the viewer's eye will automatically be drawn to the action photo. This is true even when the non action image is of a much higher photographic quality than the action one.

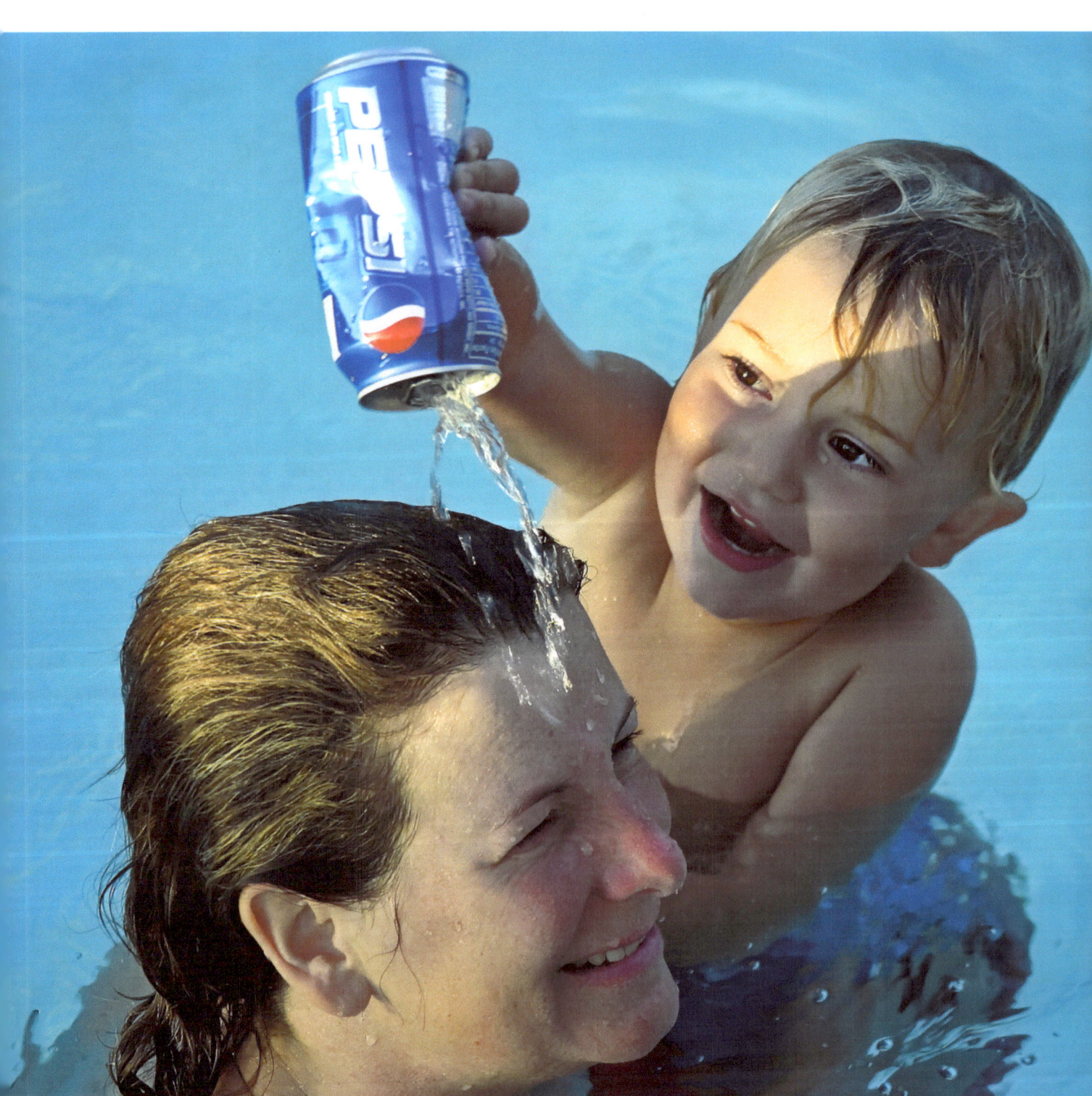

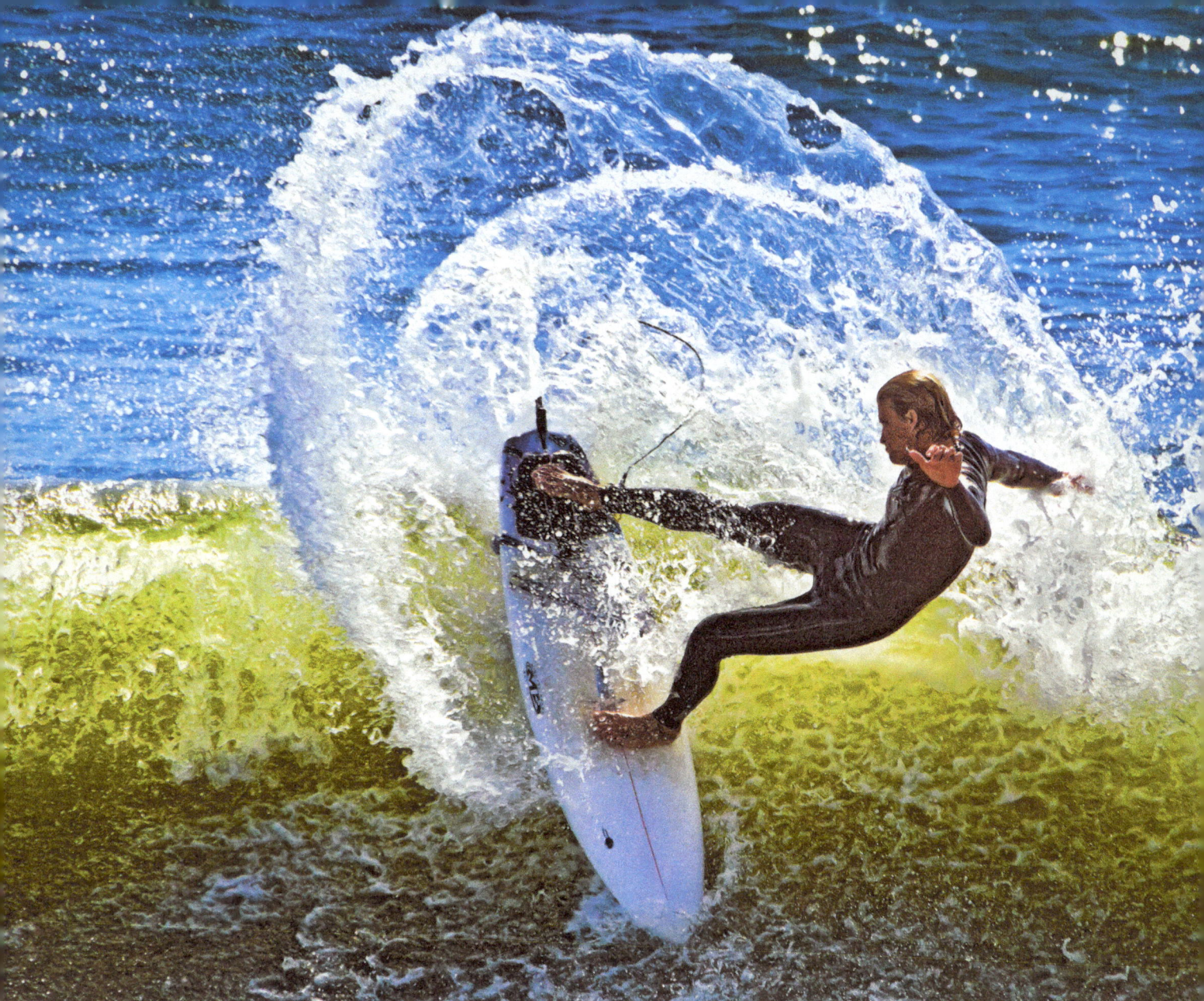

Motion is emotion. Hang loose. Enjoy life, and savor the moment!

Viewers are also more willing to overlook imperfections in action shots because:
- They become caught up in the action before they have a chance to nit pick.
- As a result of the challenges, minor imperfections are taken for granted in action photography.

The joy and the connection between the mother and child in this photo makes me smile. So does the boy's obvious glee at being daring and naughty. The light falling on his face serves to accentuate that he is the main person in the story—the doer.

I love the intensity of the surfer, the colors, the body language, and the shape of the spray.

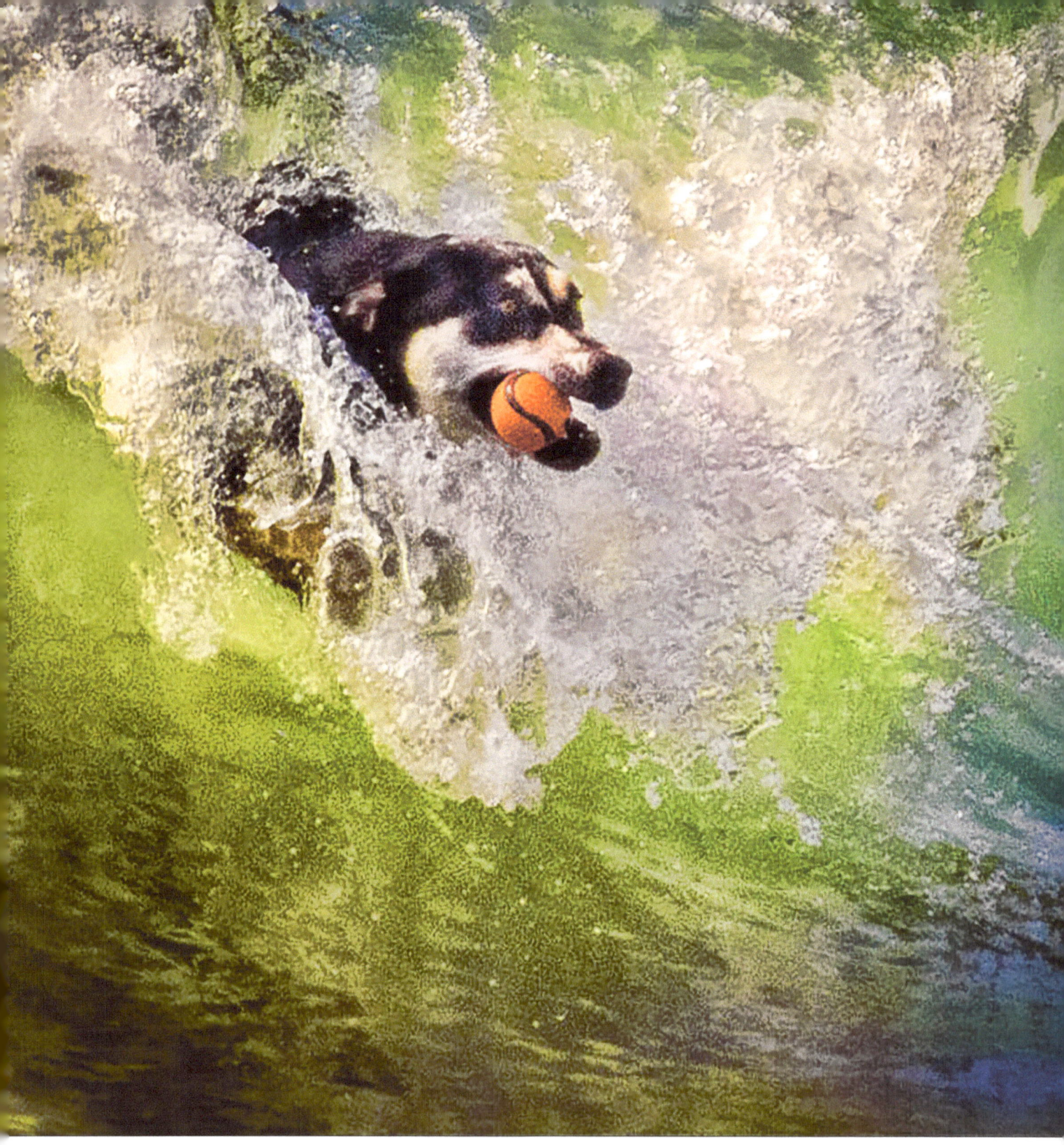

Be happy. Don't worry!

Embrace the good in your photographs. Realize that the chance of anyone producing a flawless image is smaller than the chance of winning a lottery with endless numbers rather than the usual six.

Since time is of the essence when shooting, one of the most important keys to outstanding action photography is thinking ahead and being prepared. Adjust your settings **before** you take your camera anywhere. Making decisions ahead of time will free your mind to focus only on what needs to be done at the spur of the moment.

Whereas some of the most magical action shots offer themselves spontaneously, most opportunities can be predicted by taking location, season, time of day, and the like into account. Give thought to what type of motifs you expect to encounter and how you expect the light to be. Ask yourself:

- What are you planning on using the photo for: Sale or personal? Stock or editorial? Print or screen?
- What emotions would you like to express?
- What mood are you in?
- What type of action will you be looking for?
- Will you be attending an event or will you just be wandering?
- Will your position be stationary or will you be able to change your point of view by moving around?
- Will you be likely to have the sun behind you or will it on the side, or will you be shooting into it?
- Will it be sunny, cloudy bright, overcast, rainy, snowy, or foggy?
- Will it be calm or windy?
- What is the quality of light like in the area where you are going to shoot?
- How much light will there be?
- What type of light metering will serve your purpose best?
- What type of focusing?
- Will you be using continuous shooting or single shot?

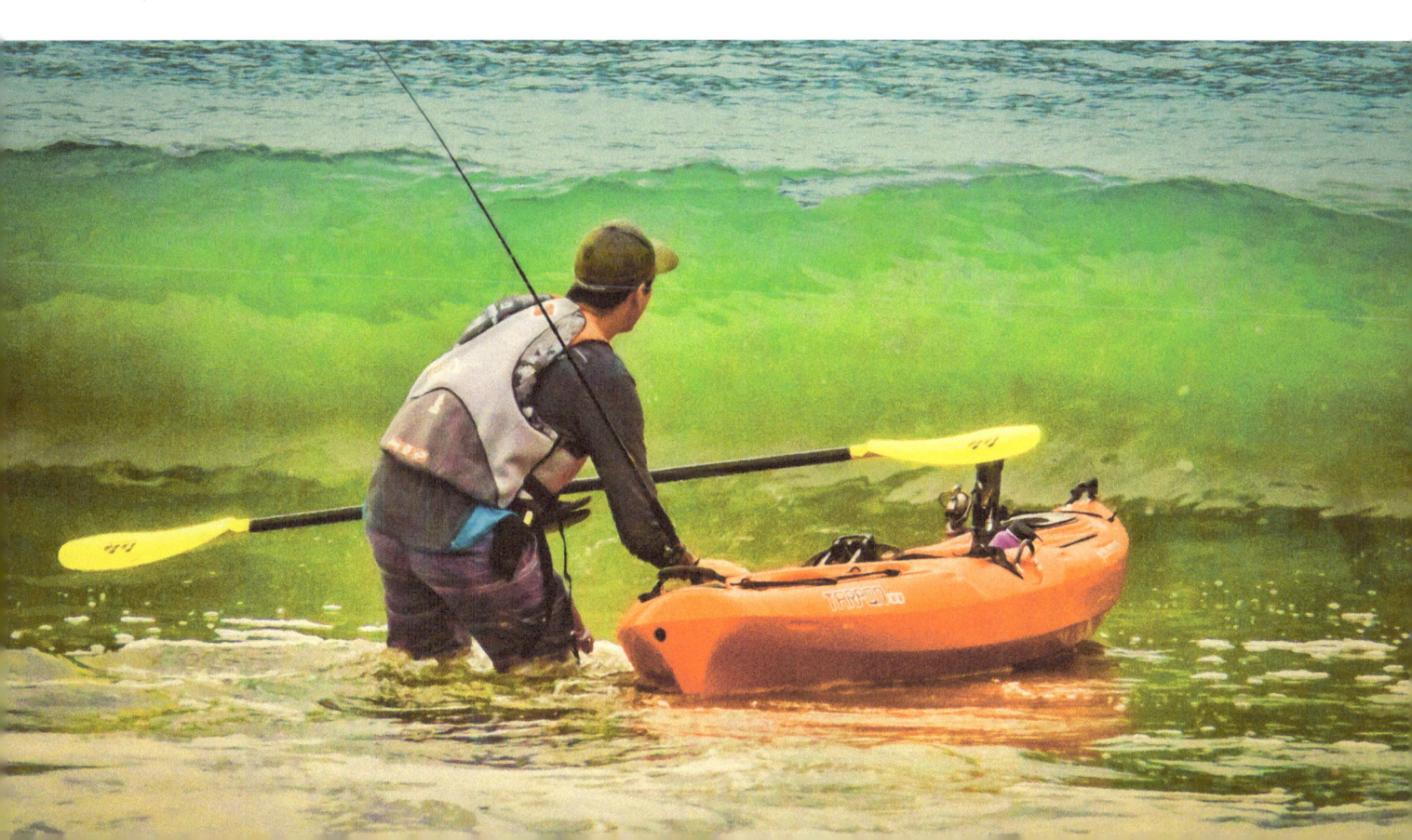

All light is not created equal! The quality and quantity of light varies according to weather, time of day, and location.

Once again—when it comes to last minute setting changes,—raw is a God send. By enabling you to change your choices after the shot, raw offers considerable leeway. So don't sweat the small stuff. Raw plugs like Adobe's Lightroom and Camera Raw are amazing. They allow photographers to make endless changes (whites, blacks, contrast, saturation and much more) in the whole picture or in smaller areas of it.

Understanding light is of utmost importance in photography. The old adage of describing photography as *painting with light* still holds even though we, today, are actually laying mosaics with pixels.

It is generally known that the weather and the time of day influences and changes the light. Everyone is aware light is starkest at midday and prettiest at sunrise and sunset. What is not so obvious is that the quantity and quality of light changes according to location. Unlike a camera, the human eye is able to adapt to light changes. Therefore we generally don't notice alterations unless they are massive or we make a point of constantly being consciously aware of them.

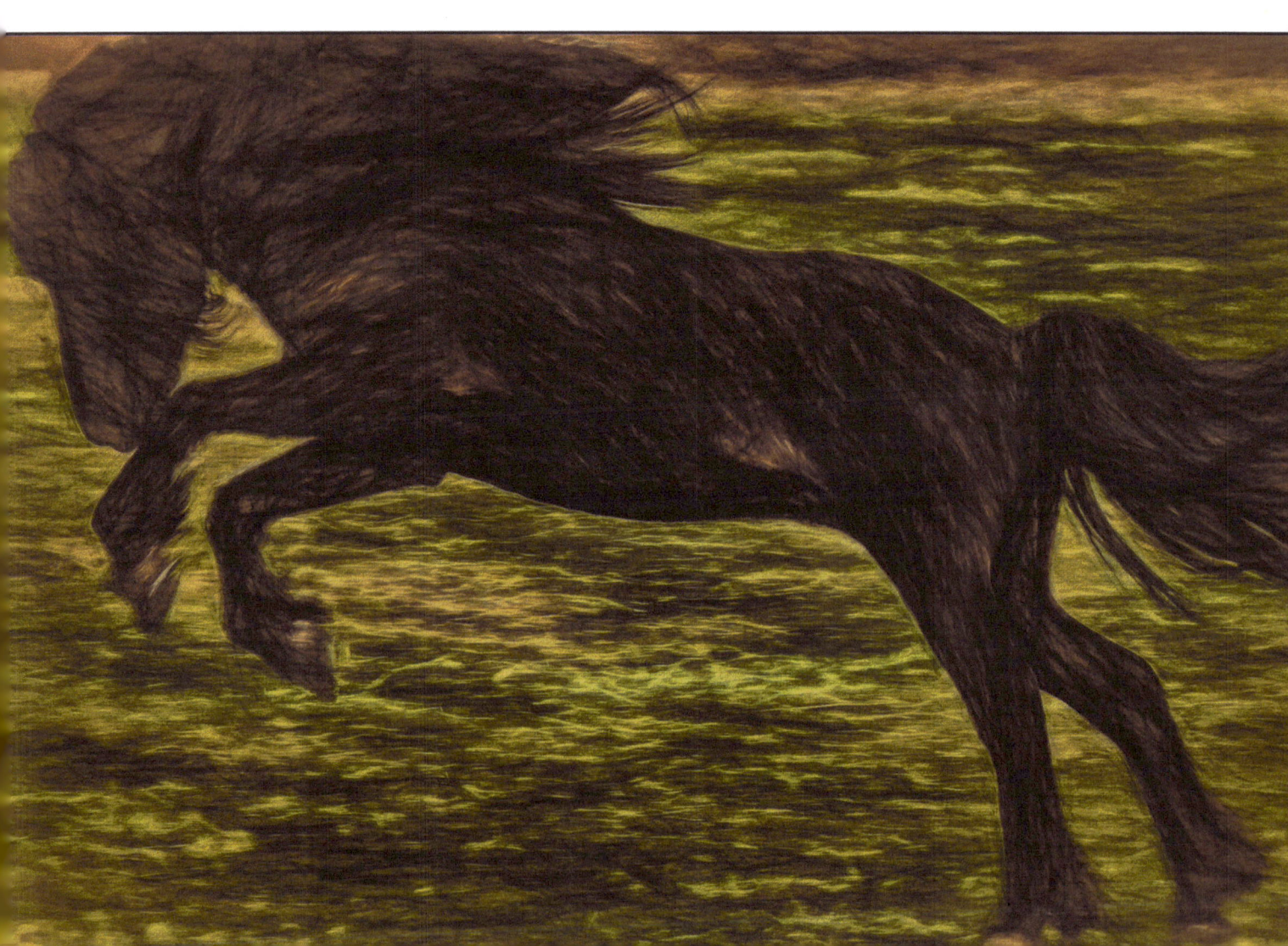

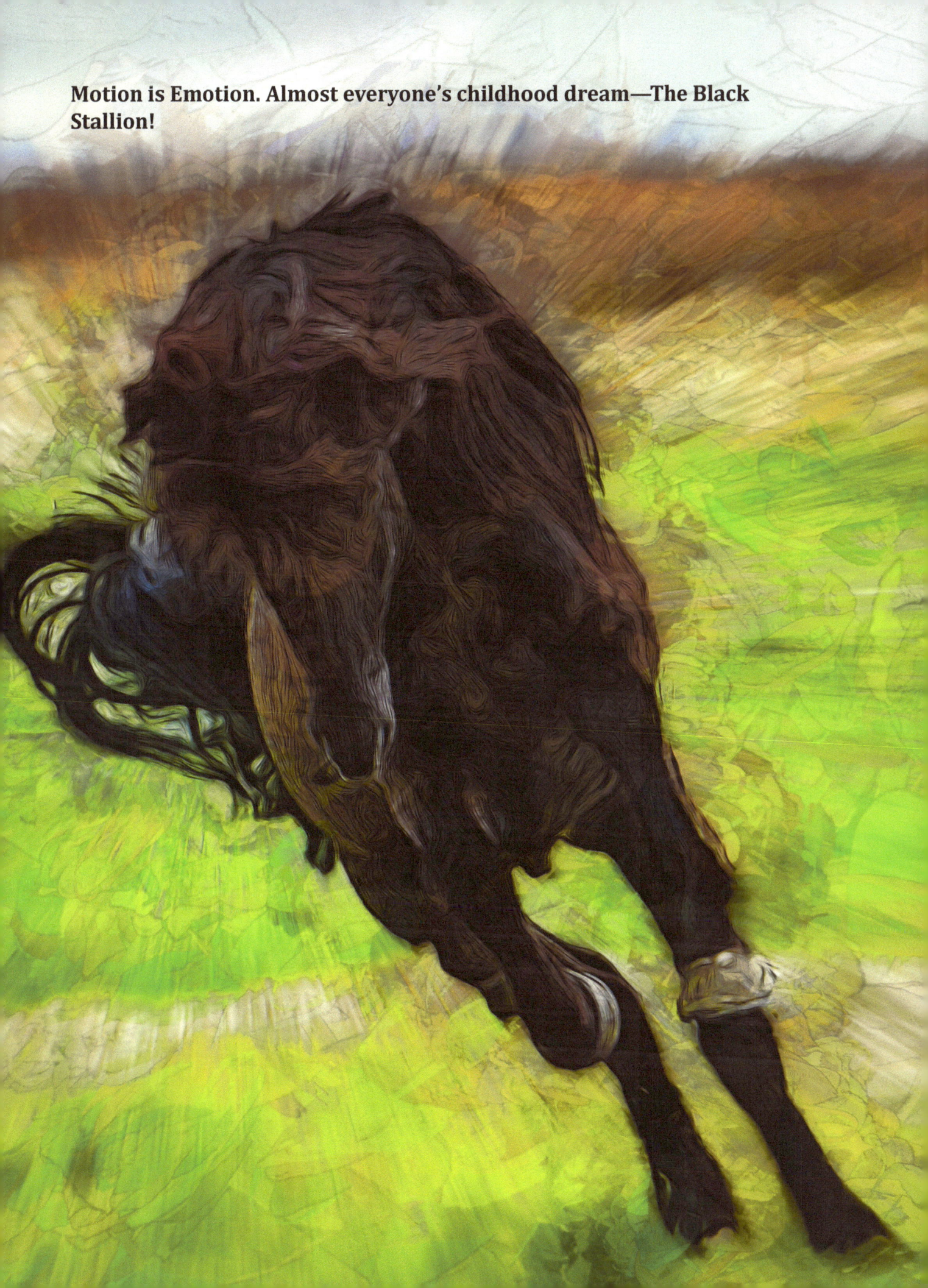

Motion is Emotion. Almost everyone's childhood dream—The Black Stallion!

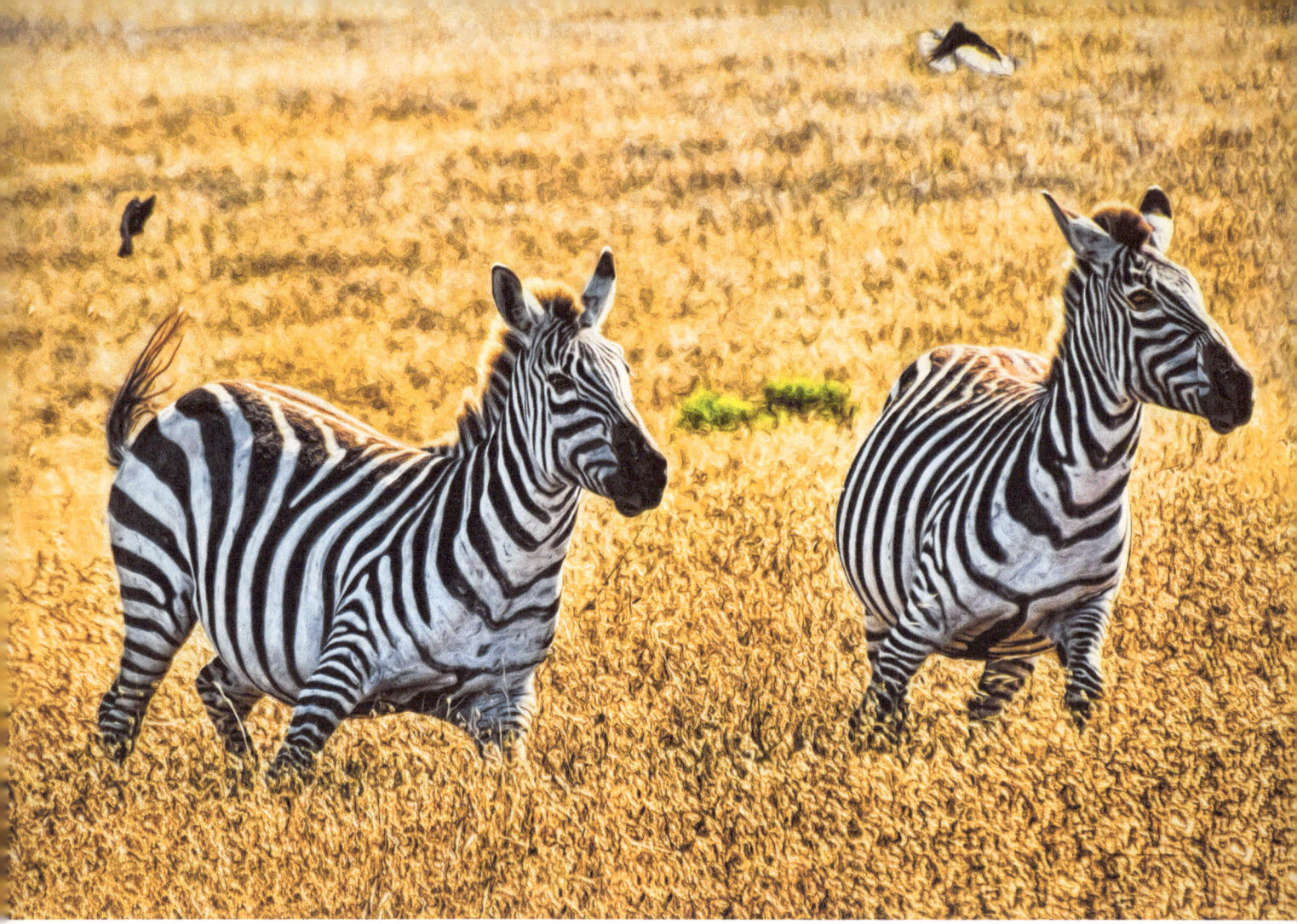

Believe in yourself! Aim for the stars. Aim for consistently awesome photography rather than one great photograph once in a while.

Generally, the closer you are to the equator and the lower humidity in the air, the starker the light and the more of it. Equally, the further you are away from the equator and the higher the humidity, the softer the light and the less of it. Additionally, mountains, forests, and buildings cast shadows that lessen and soften the light. Altitude also matters as does time of year.

The change can be quite marked even over small distances. Directly on the ocean where I live—in Cambria in Central California—the light is soft enough that you can get wonderful exposures year around all day long. Only 25 miles inland—in Paso Robles—the light is much starker and photographing in the middle of the day can be problematic.

In Iceland—the land of the midnight sun—early morning and late evening light is incredibly soft and beautiful. Unfortunately—even though the light seems bright to the naked eye—it is wise to keep a close eye on ISO. Often, when the light is at its prettiest, there is not enough of it to successfully action freeze at acceptable ISO.

Unlike what one might imagine, the photos on this spread are not from the African Savannah, but taken from Highway 1 adjacent to the 225,000 acre Hearst Ranch on the California Central Coast. Huge herds of zebras roam freely here—remnants of Randolf Heart's Castle zoo.

The main challenge to photographing them is that you have to do so from the road on the outside of the fence. This means you must be in luck and/or wait for them to show up. Furthermore, this limits how close you can get to the herds and from which direction you can shoot them. Do you have photo opps like that?

We tend to see the black and white zebra stripes as very striking. And it is only when you begin seeing your results after photographing them, that you realize that the function of the stripes is really camouflage. Getting the zebras to stand out from the tall grasses is difficult unless they are close to the fence. Do you have any wild life sanctuaries close to your home that you have not visited yet?

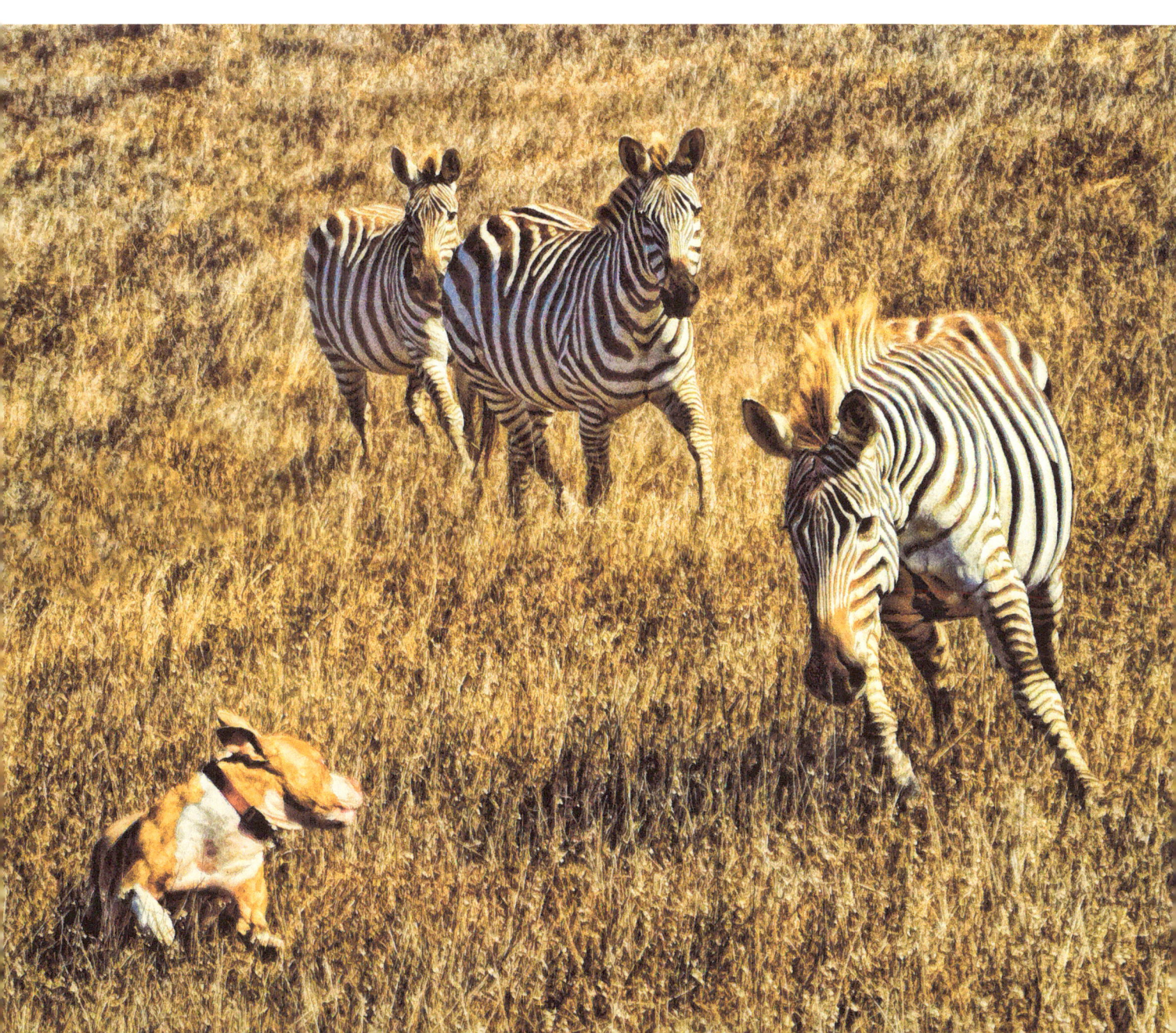

Shoot from the hip and be fast on the draw. When in doubt, shoot!

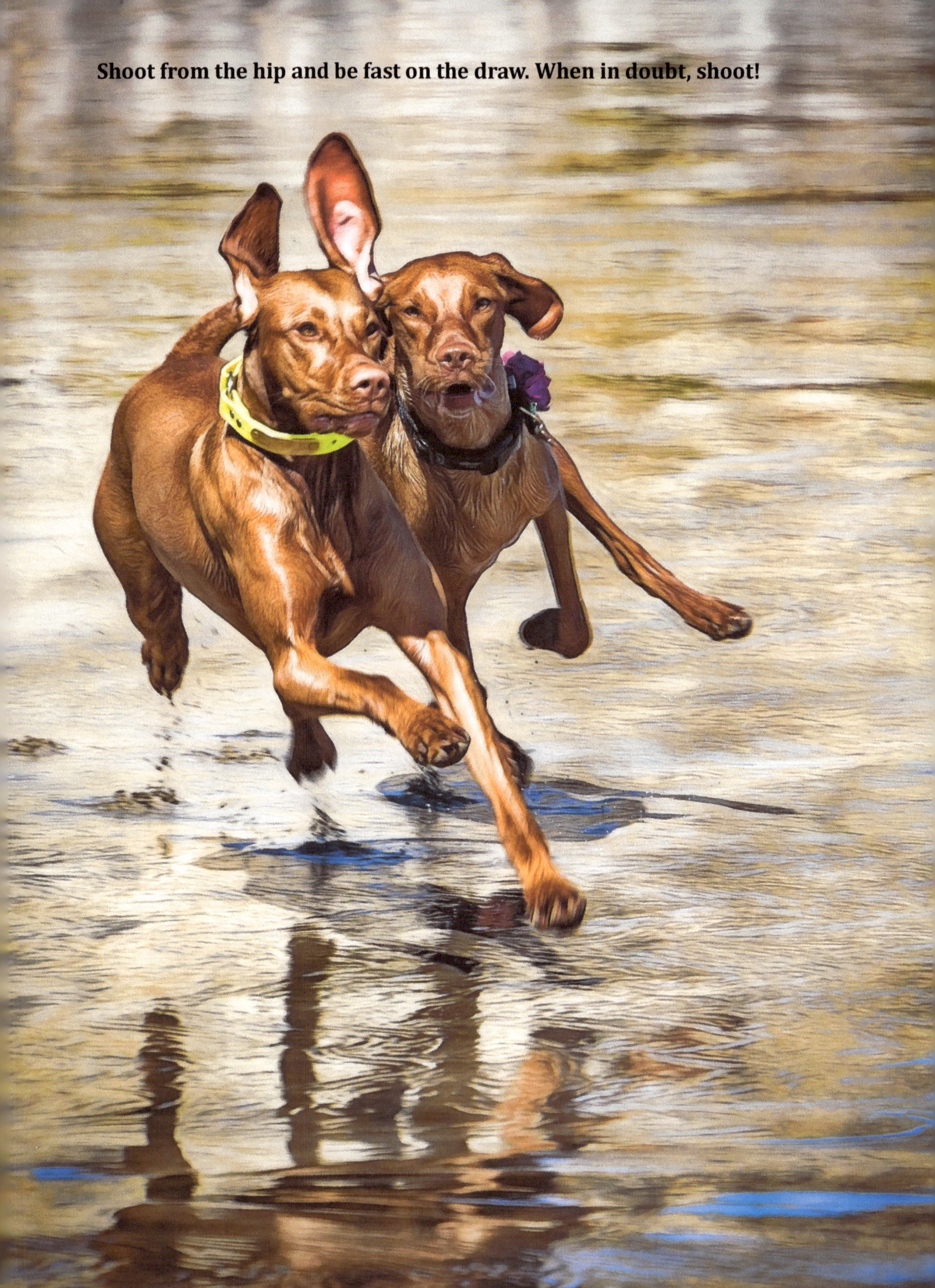

What other tricks are important to action photography in general and to action freezes specifically?

- Focus on, and begin following, the action—exactly pacing it—as soon as possible. Simultaneously frame and create your composition. Anticipate the motion pattern.
- Start shooting as soon as you are in tune with the "dance". Develop a the shooting rhythm that will result in you clicking at the desired point of the action. Keep up the rhythm until the object in action has fully passed you. Doing so will ensure you don't delay for a split second at the critical moment. Don't worry about the unneeded shots. Delete buttons on computers are easy to find and who knows? One of the extra shots could be a winner.
- Understand lag time—the same type of delay that occurs between your decision to brake your car and it actually begins slowing. Be aware that there will always be a short delay between the time you decide to fire and the time when the camera actually shoots. Lag time is the sum of yours and the camera's reaction time.

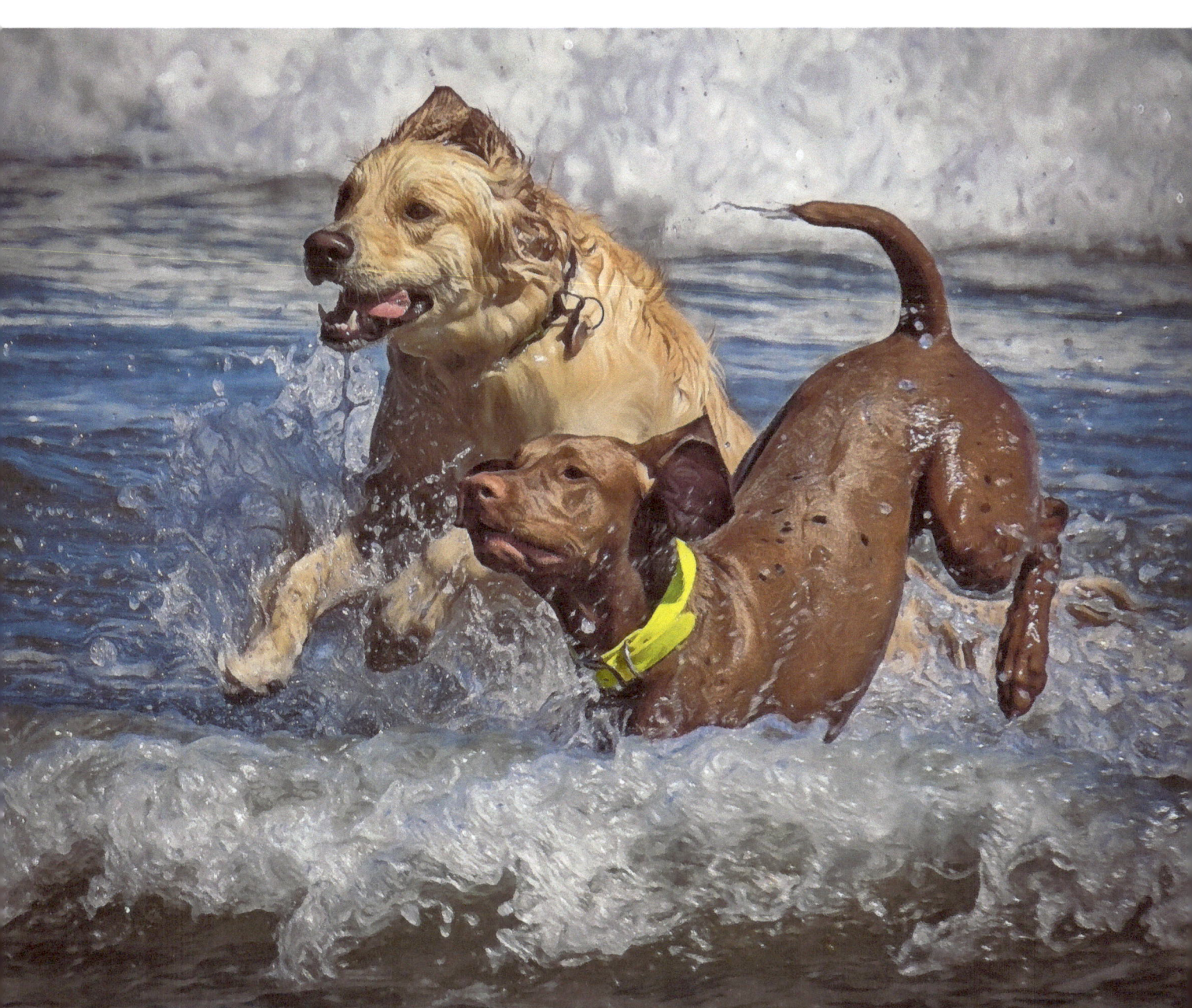

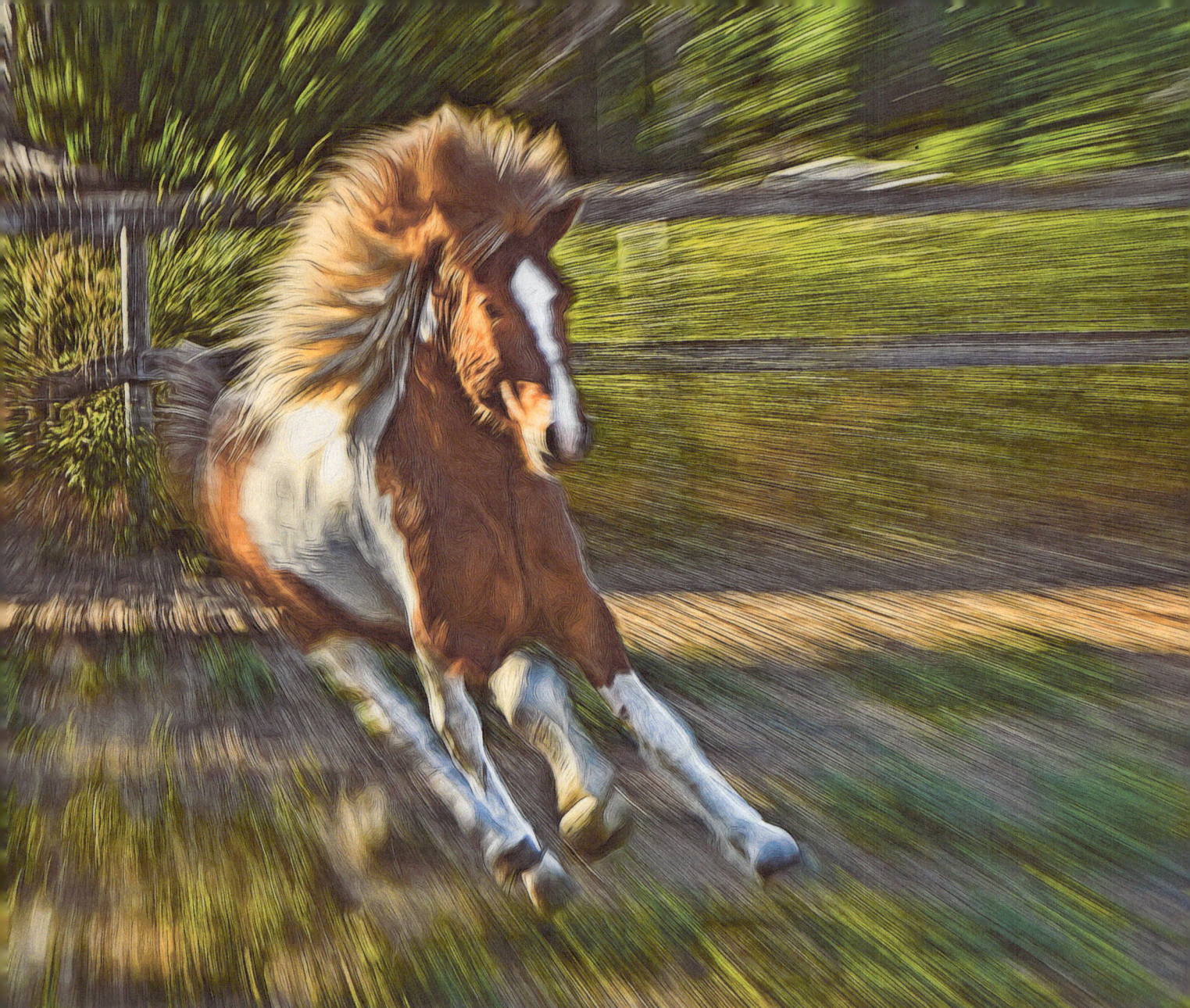

Slow speed blurs and zoom blurs are fun but tricky. Both offer the possibility of some very interesting images. The criteria for slow speed blurs is slow shutter speed. Otherwise everything goes. Experiment! Try a variety of speeds and camera movements.

Zoom blur is created at slow shutter speed by the moving object coming towards you. Some photographers add to the effect by zooming the lens closer during the process.

The blur in both of the photos on this spread are created in camera. The horses are Icelandic, but I shot them during a photo shoot at a friend's ranch in Central California.

To me photos like these blurs are just the icing on the cake—something to play with when you have covered what else you set out to do. Also, this type of shot is most often the result of failure to accomplish something else you set out to do.

The drawback to both of the techniques is that you have very little control, making results very difficult to predict. Nowadays, we have endless opportunities to experiment photographically—not only in camera, but also afterwards on the computer. The easiest and most fool proof way to create zoom blur and slow speed blur photos is to do so in a photo editing program.

Mix and match blur filters to create slow speed blur. Be creative! When "artificially" generating zoom blur, two things are important—the strength of the filter and where you place the focus of the blur. The strength is obviously a matter of taste, but the focus of the blur generally works best, when placed on the point of interest of the photo. (Each brand of filter is different but more advanced software will provide you with a way of choosing the focus point.)

Imagine, envision, experiment, play, and create! Realize that you— just like you have to kiss a lot of toads before you find your prince—have to shoot a lot of duds before you win the photographic jackpot.

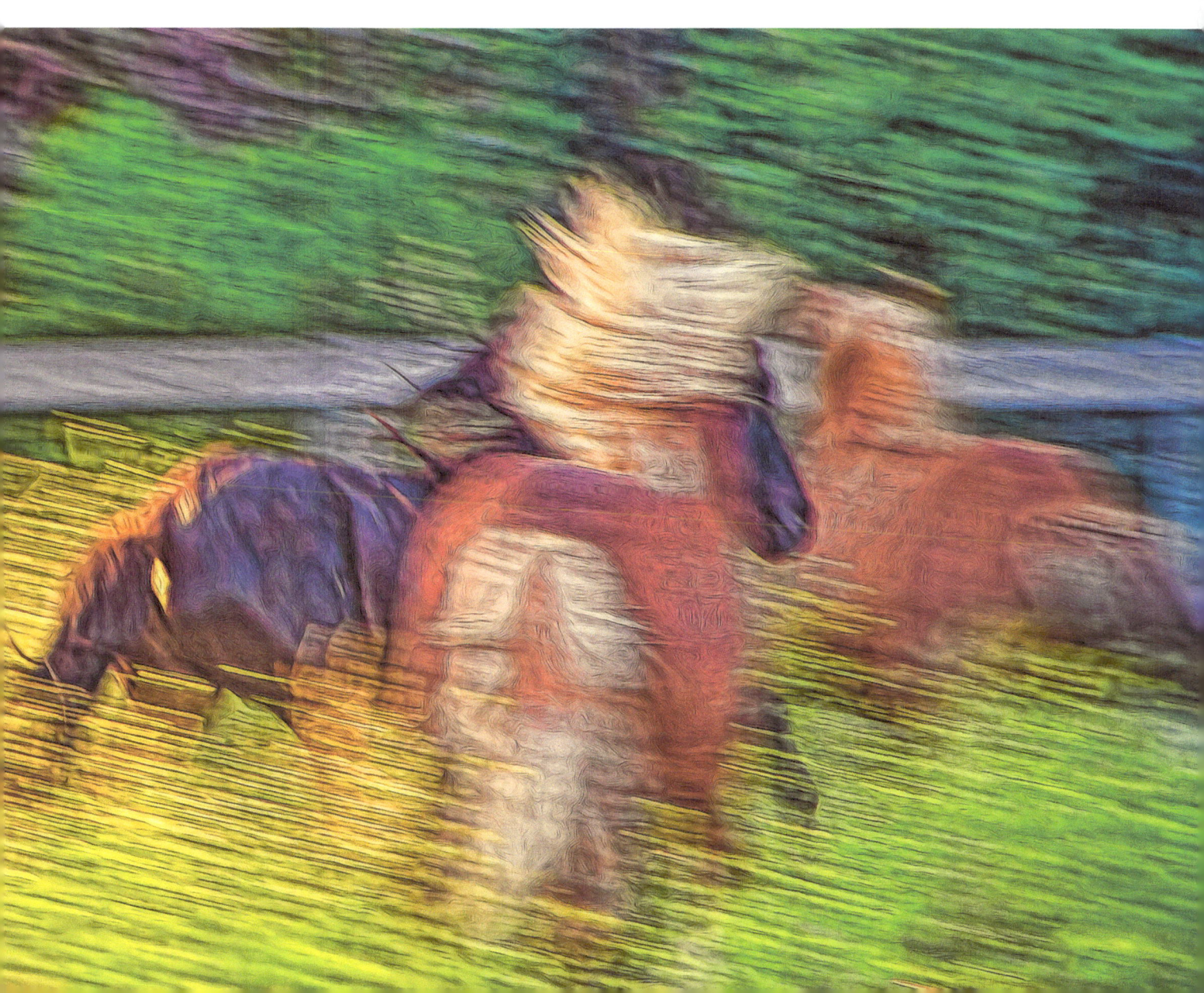

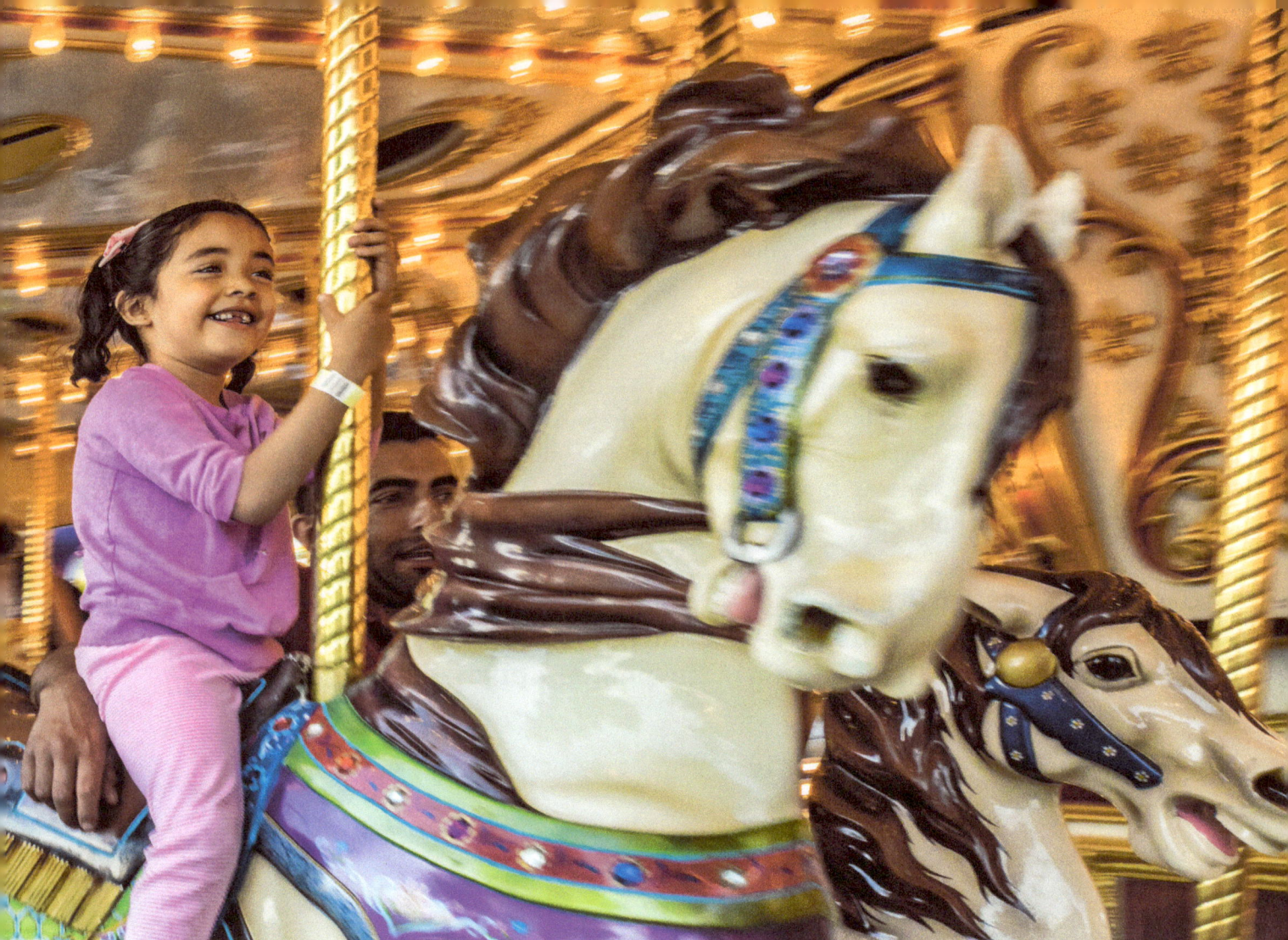

Panning is the most fun, and the most attention getting action photography technique. It is relatively easy to learn and the results (if you take enough pictures) are predictable. Just like slow speed and zoom blur pans can be created in computer

The photography method is the same as the one suggested for motion freeze except for the slow shutter speed and the importance of keeping your camera parallel to the area you want to be in focus—the action's point of interest. Vary your shutter speed according to the speed of the moving object, the complexity of the background, and on how streaky you want your finished product to be. Start out with faster shutter speeds and go slower as you become more proficient. Keep your shutter speed within a range from 1/60 second to 1/25 of a seconds. Faster shutter speeds have little effect and will just look like the photos are accidentally blurry. Very slow shutter speeds generally create nasty background streaks.

Realize that all the parts of the moving object may not move in the same direction or at the same speed—think pedals on bicycle, individually moving animal legs, carousel horses moving up and down as well as forward. Choose which part of the object is most important and concentrate on keeping just that in focus.

Develop your eye! Widen your point of view.

Both of the photos on this spread are pans. The one to the left was taken at a recent county fair on the California Central Coast. The one to the left was shot many years ago at a Kentucky race track.

The challenge in panning the carousel was the circular rather than the parallel movement. Here again it was important to start following the action as soon as the subject came into view.

The focus on the front horse in the background is probably not optimal. I spent quite some time deliberating whether I was okay with it. Finally I decided that perhaps—in its own way—it added to the picture.

The interesting thing about the racing photo is its focus. The horses are most likely in the home stretch where the jockeys fight to catch up with and pass the horses on the inside rail. This causes only some of the horses to be sharp. I find that okay with, too.

The straight line of the rail and the forward leaning position of the jockeys show us direction. Nonetheless it is the position of the legs of the horses in the foreground that are the icing on the cake.

The reason the photo works so well—despite the horses having almost passed the photographer and the viewer—is that the race is on. They are going somewhere and we want to go there with them.

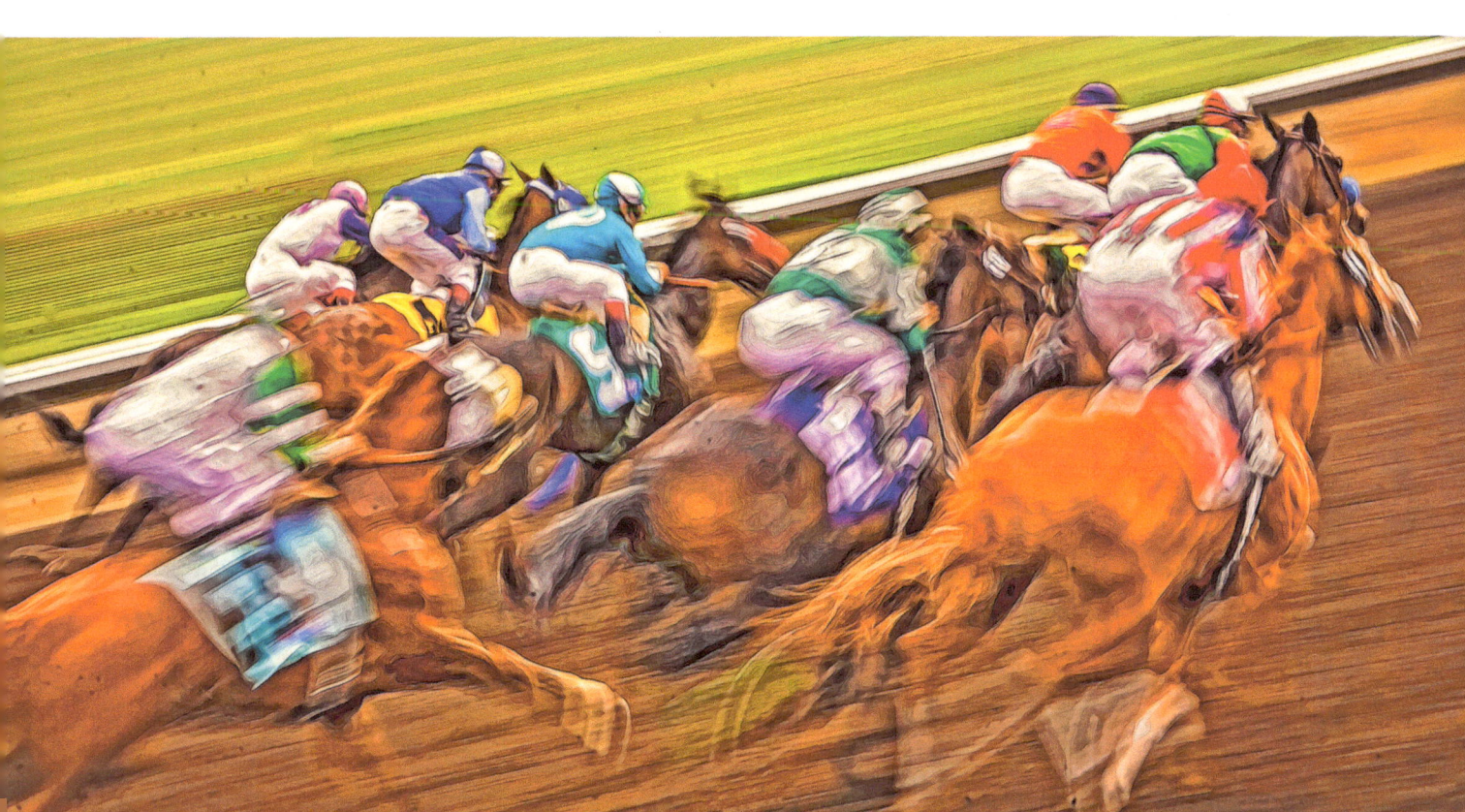

Decide on your point of focus ahead of time or as soon as the moving object comes into view. Keeping the area you consider most important in focus will tell the viewer what part of the photo is the point of interest.

A useful technique when panning is to pretend to be videoing the procession rather than photographing it. Start moving your camera with the motion immediately your point of interest comes into view. Allow yourself all the possible time to correctly pace yourself and to compose your shots. Prevent yourself from freezing up at the critical moment by starting a sequence of "warm up" clicks way before the subject is in the right position. These shots are not meant to be used. (Using the delete button will easily get rid of them after the fact.) Use the continuous shoot setting and take as may exposures as possible while the subject is within the correct range.

The composition of the photo—the positioning of the point of interest—is very important. Use the rule of thirds and be aware that it is a part of our human nature to feel more connected to objects moving towards us than to those moving away. Keep clicking even after the subject has passed, but do so only to make sure you don't loose your momentum too early. Once an object has passed viewers loose interest. The only thing that overrides position is foot-fall. Objects in an unbalanced position make viewers feel uncomfortable.

Background is important in photo pans. They add to the story, without overpowering the subject. You can successfully pan on any background. But remember it is the streaks that add a sense of motion. If you shoot on a totally bland background, you won't get any streaks and you might as well have saved yourself the trouble and frozen the picture.

The pans on the page to the right are from Landsmot—The National Championships for Icelandic Horses in Iceland. Here, a long stride, a high leg lift, and clear beat are very important criteria for winning. Notice that Icelandic Horses have a different foot-fall than most other horses. It is a four-beat gait. Icelanders call it toelt. Other laterally gaited breeds use different terms for the sequence—single-foot, rack, paso liano, and amble.

What I like about the photo on top of the page is the color and stance of the horse, the obvious power in the hind part, the long stride, the high leg lift, and the natural headset. I feel the pan adds a sense of motion and makes the horse stand out form the background..

I appreciate the photo below for the same reasons. Furthermore, I enjoy the blurred TV photographer. I believe he gives a fun sense of place. Thirdly I like the position and synchronicity of the horses. All are in the same phase of movement. The horses are spaced evenly on a pleasing diagonal line. Each horse's head can be seen clearly as can those of the riders.

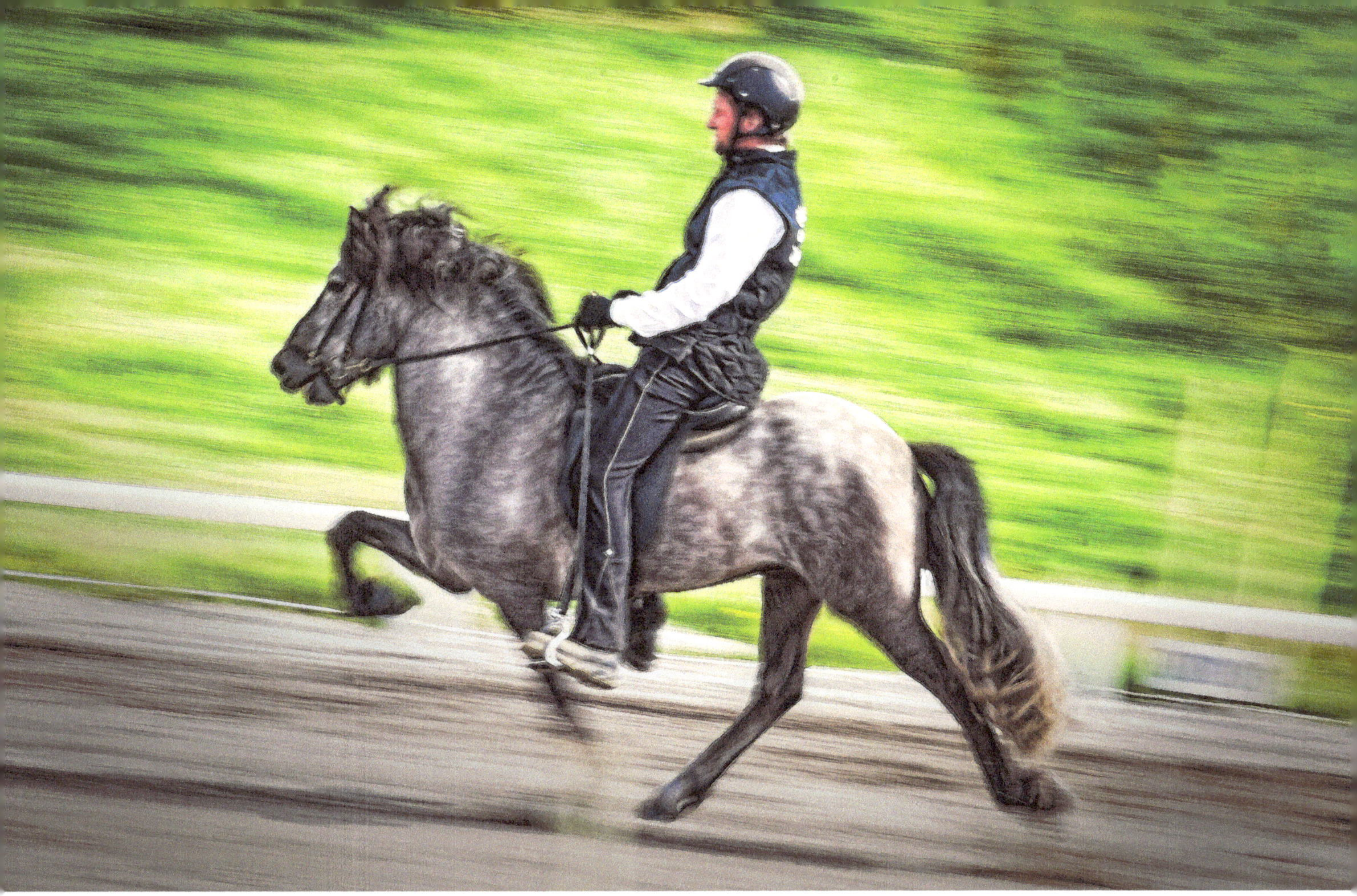

Whatever got you to where you are today, will not get you where you want to be tomorrow!

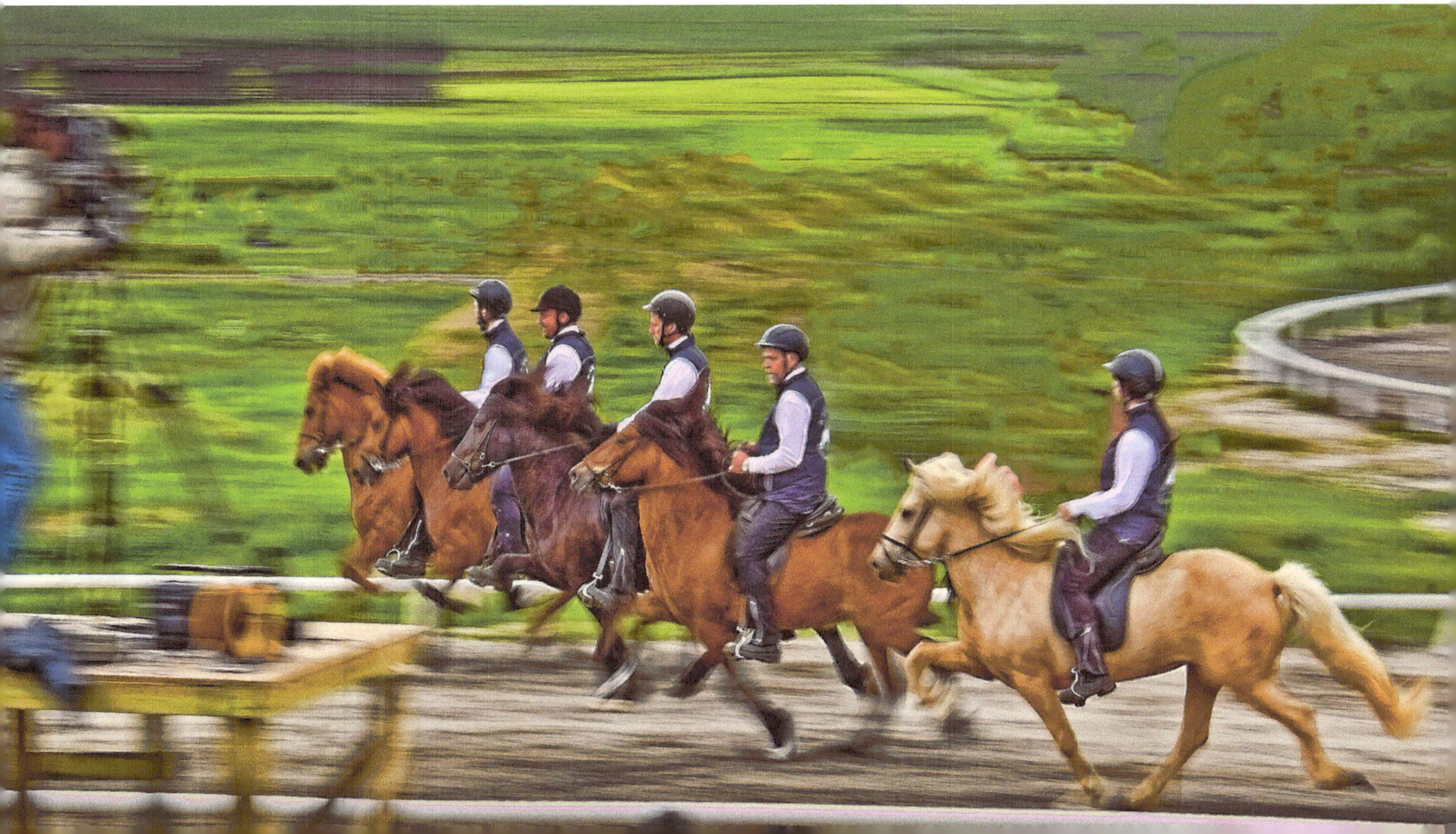

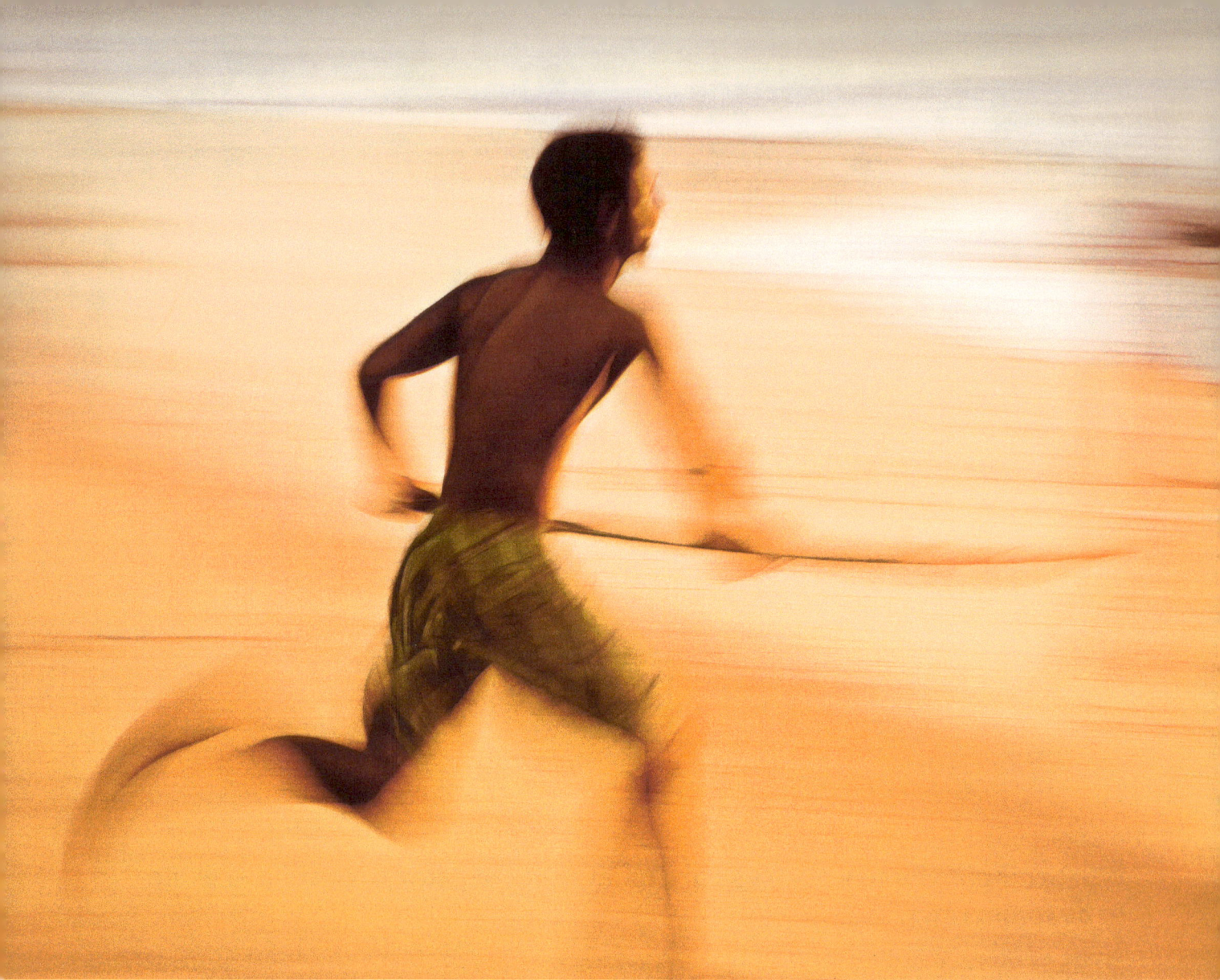

Be proactive rather than reactive. Stay ahead of the wave.

The surfing photos on this spread are both taken in Carlsbad in Southern California. The picture on the left hand page is a pan and the one on the right is partly a pan and partly a slow shutter speed blur. Together with the warm colors, the strong shapes, and the clear leading lines, the techniques results in two unusual images.

Creating a theme that ties in with the country you are visiting is a useful trick in travel photography. I created the pans in the composite on the next spread while visiting Copenhagen, Denmark a decade or so ago. I walked about the city for an hour or two having great fun panning bicycles and their riders.

Just like Holland, Denmark is known for its many bicycles and I feel these pans offer a great sense of place. What I enjoy most about the images is the obvious individuality and personality of the riders.

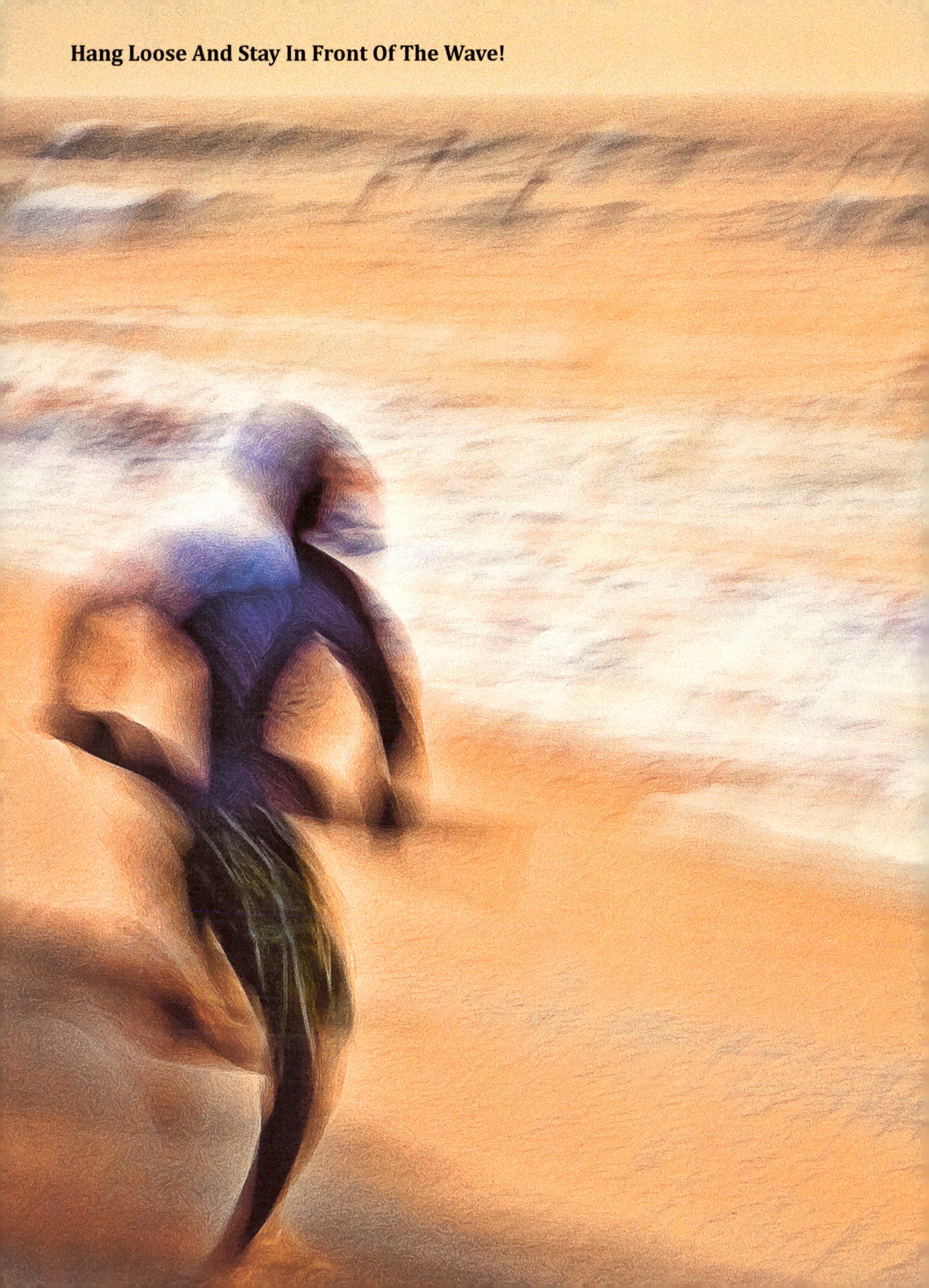

Hang Loose And Stay In Front Of The Wave!

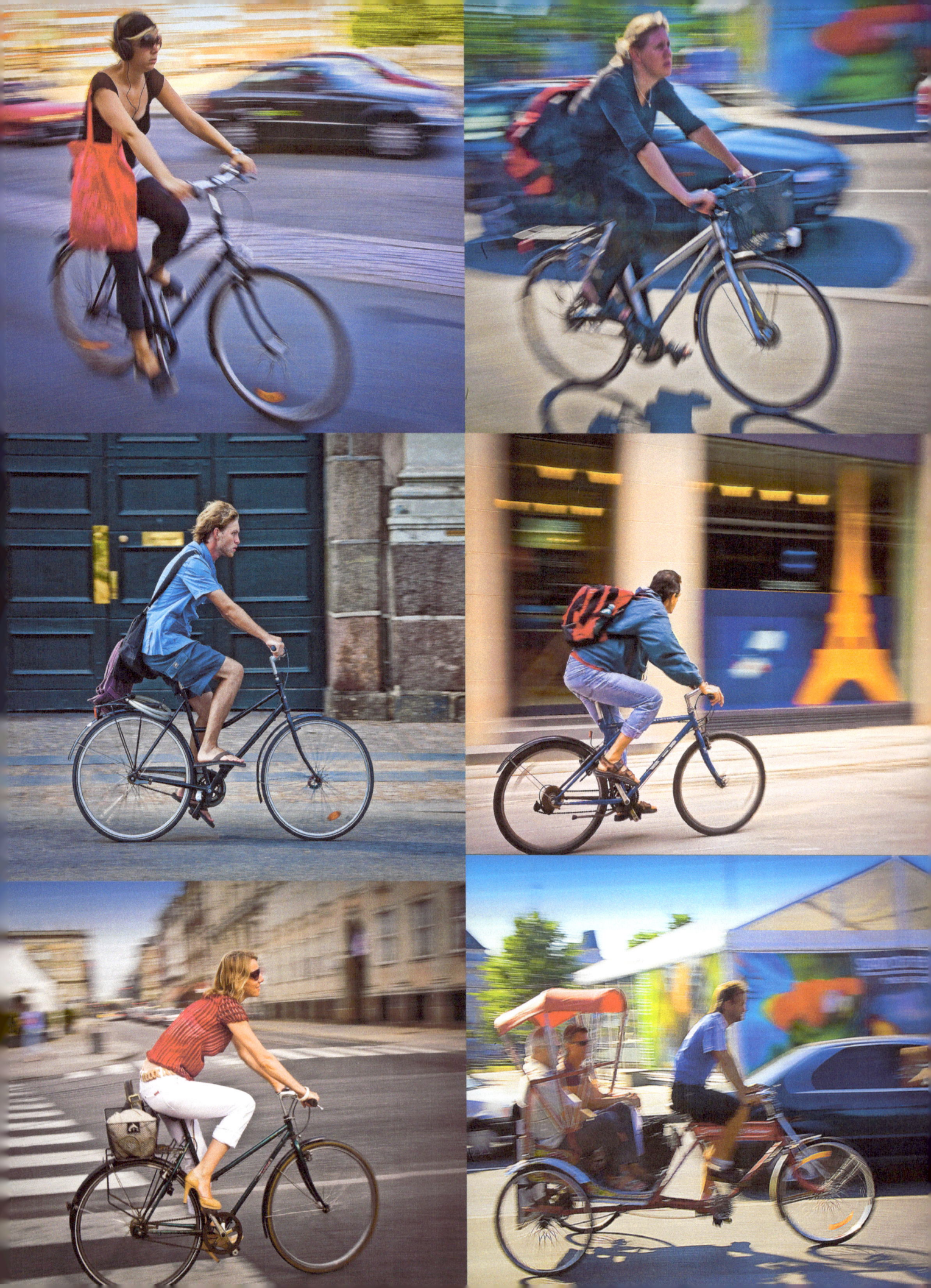

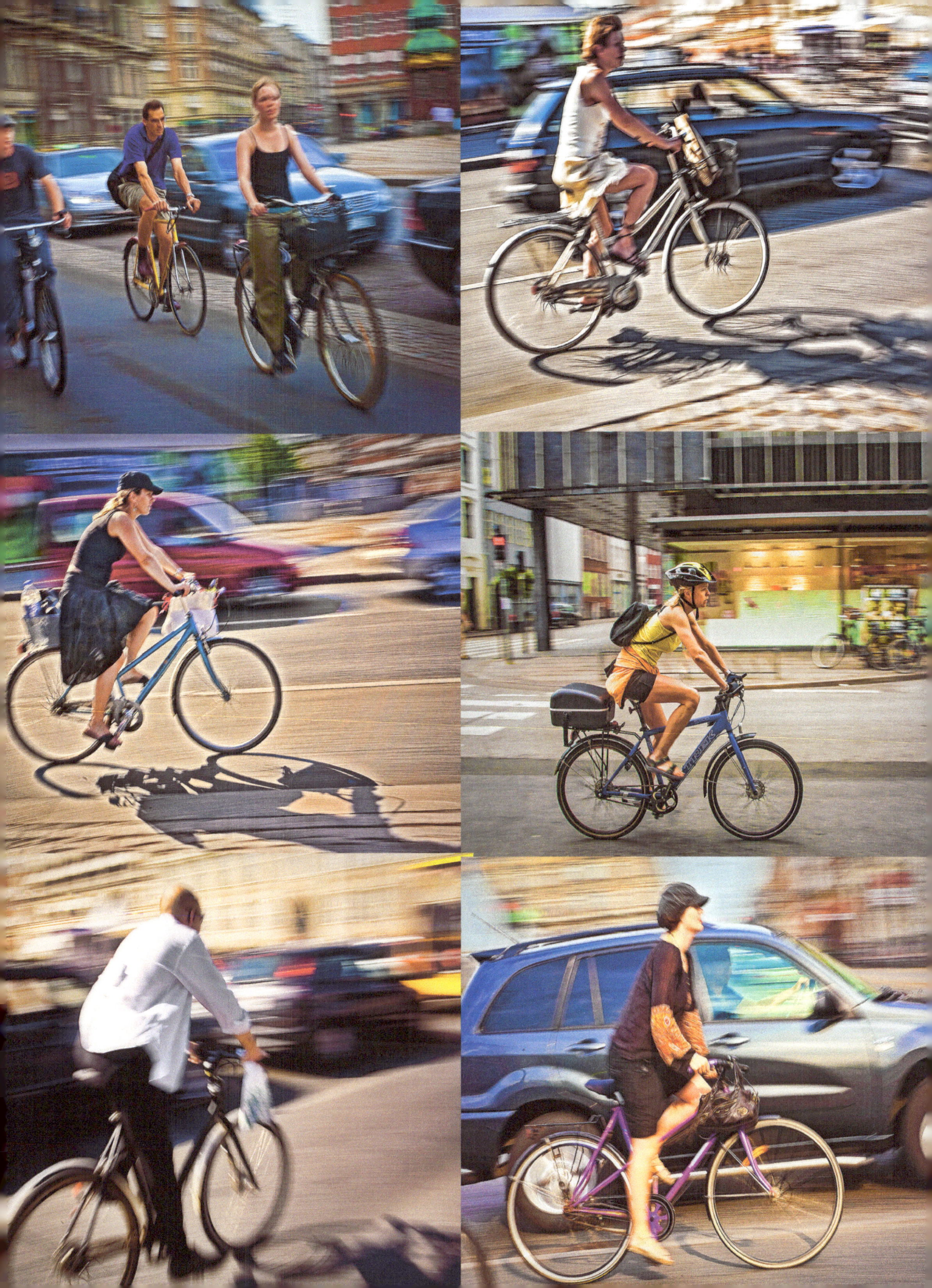

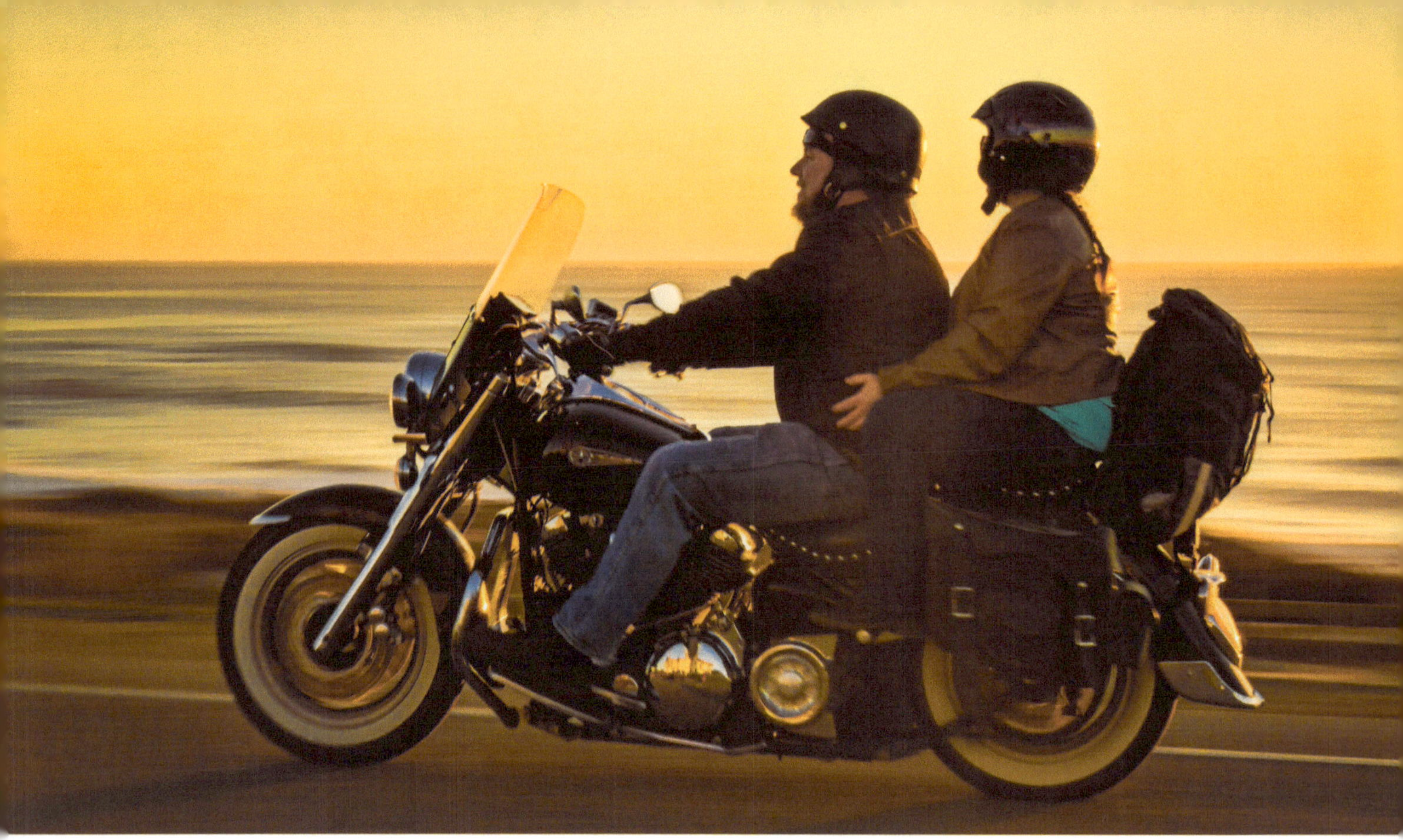

I panned the photos on this spread last night while I did my usual sunset walk along Moonstone Beach, in Cambria, Central Coast California. I had three reasons for shooting them.

- I wanted to amuse and entertain myself.
- Panning cars and bikes is good target practice.
- I was looking for some useful shots to include in this book. I wanted to show just how interesting panned images of easy, mundane subjects can be.

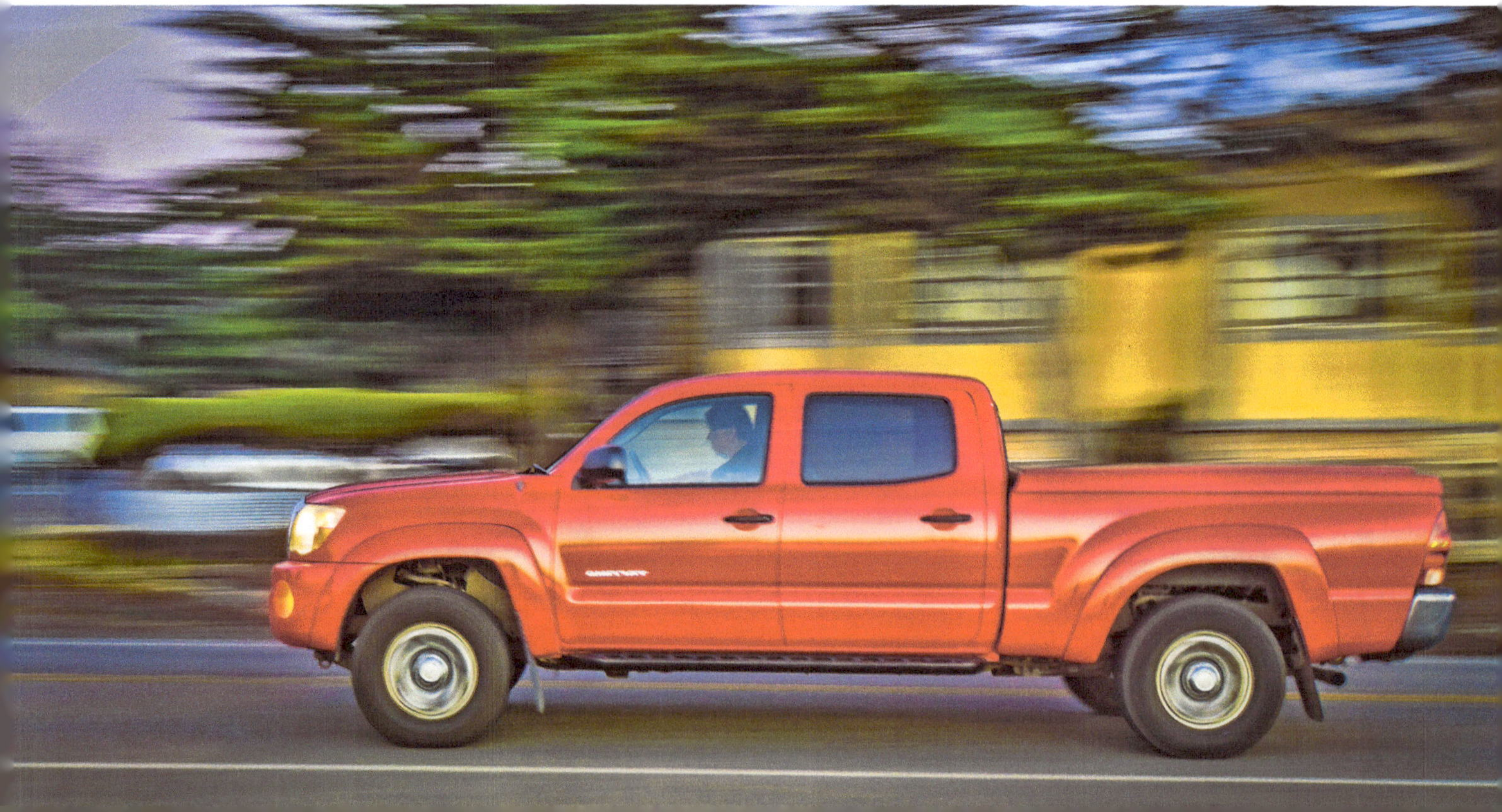

When you first get into panning, start with easy subjects like cars, trains, and bicycles that move at a given speed in a set, straight direction. Have fun with the process. Experiment with light, composition, and color. When you do so, commonplace action can lead to striking photos.

Don't worry if you don't get all your panning ducks in a row right away. Panning is just like driving a car. The first few times are stressful. Your reactions are slow, and you have to think all the time. Then—all of a sudden—everything falls in place and the process becomes automatic.

Remember, that just like you have to kiss a lot of toads before you find your prince, you will get a considerable amount of duds when you first start panning. Hang loose and don't worry. Be happy!

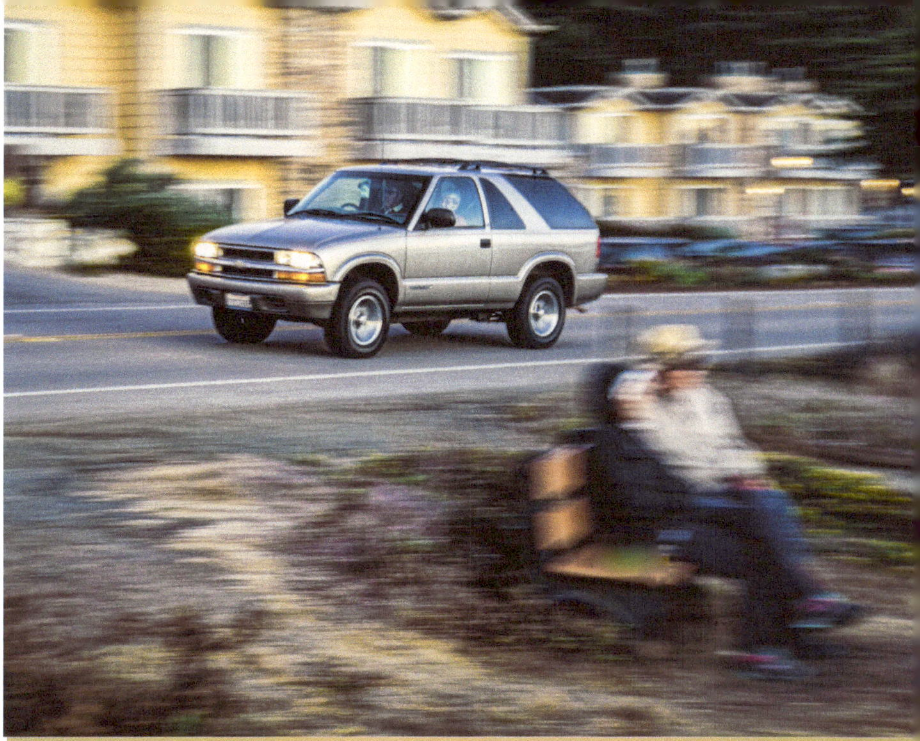

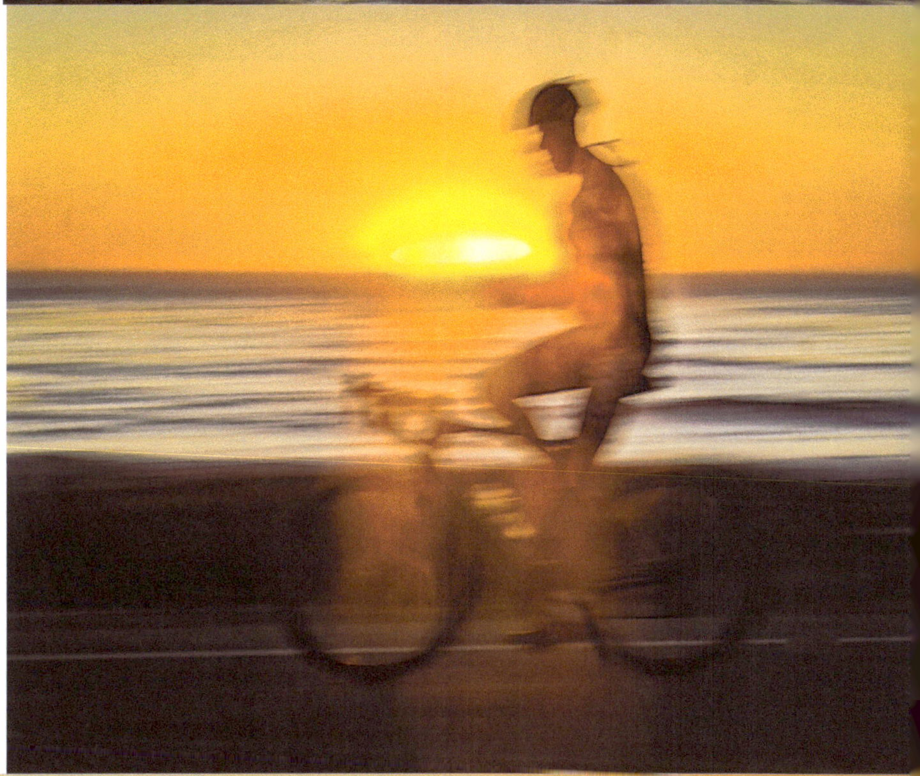

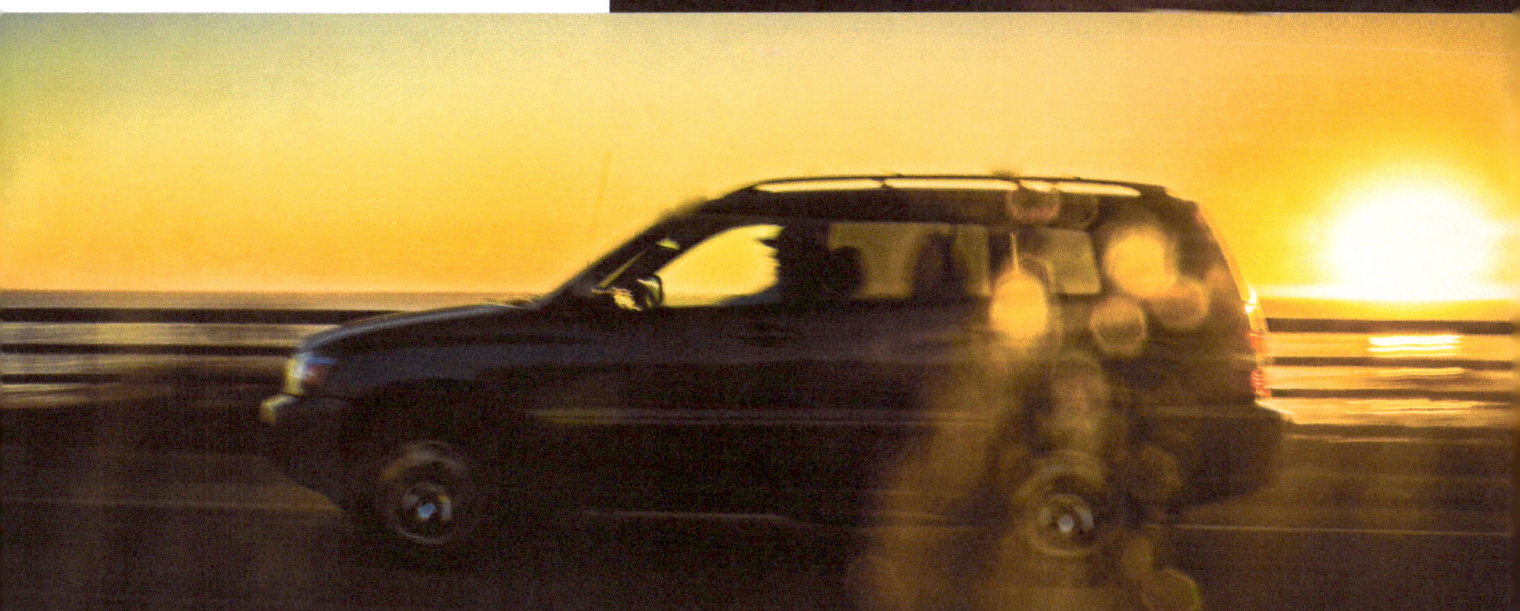

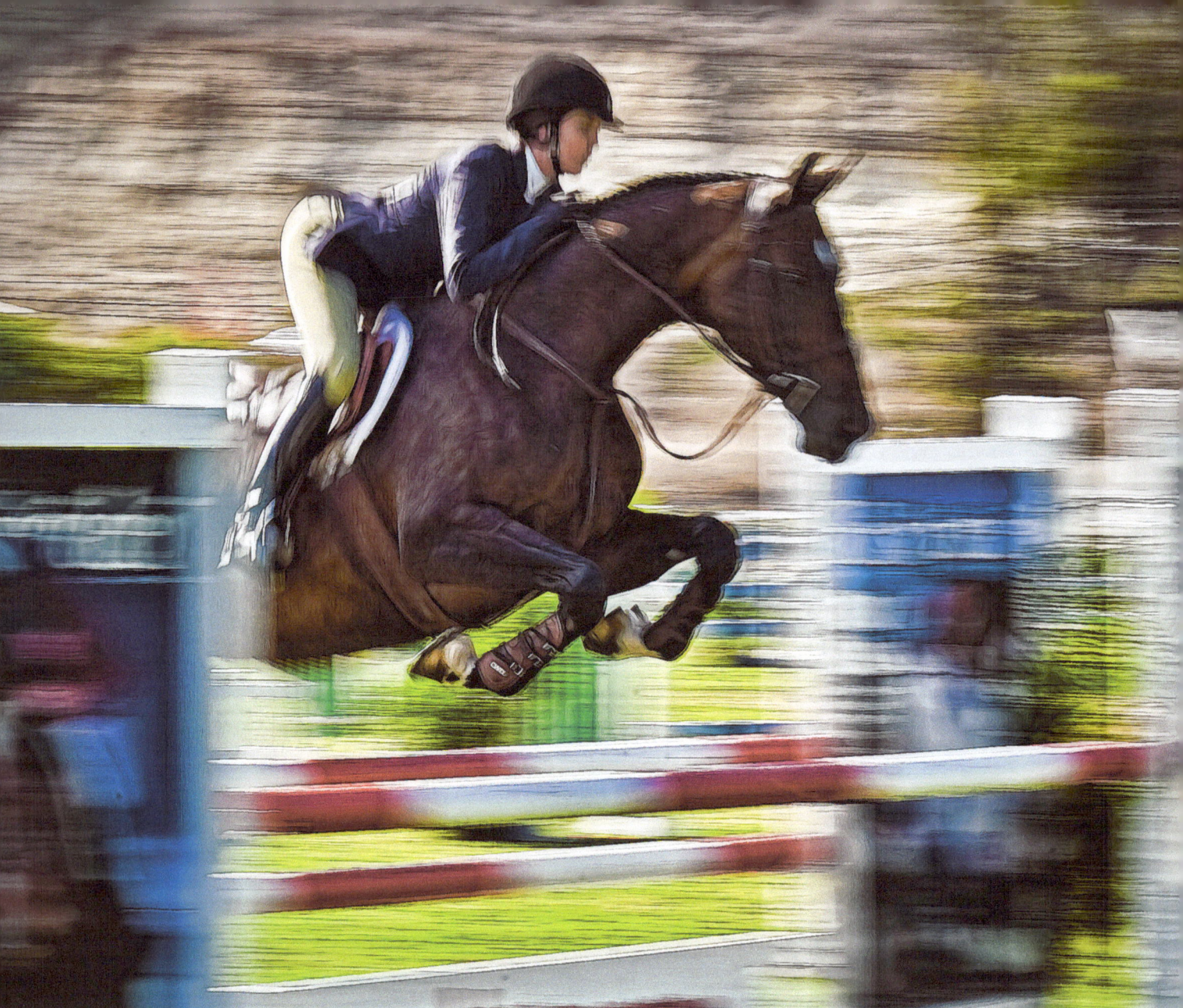

At first glance, the photos on this spread appear to be quite difficult to accomplish. Actually they are easier to shoot than most other pans of moving animals.

I took the pictures at a high level show jumping show in Southern California, standing perpendicular to the jumps in the spectator area.

Because of the expertise of the competitors, the timing and movement of the horses was very predictable once you understood the pattern. They would all accelerate towards the jump, take off in the correct spot, tuck their front legs and fly. All I had to do was to follow their movement and click at the peak moment.

Are there any interesting events for you to photograph close to where you live?

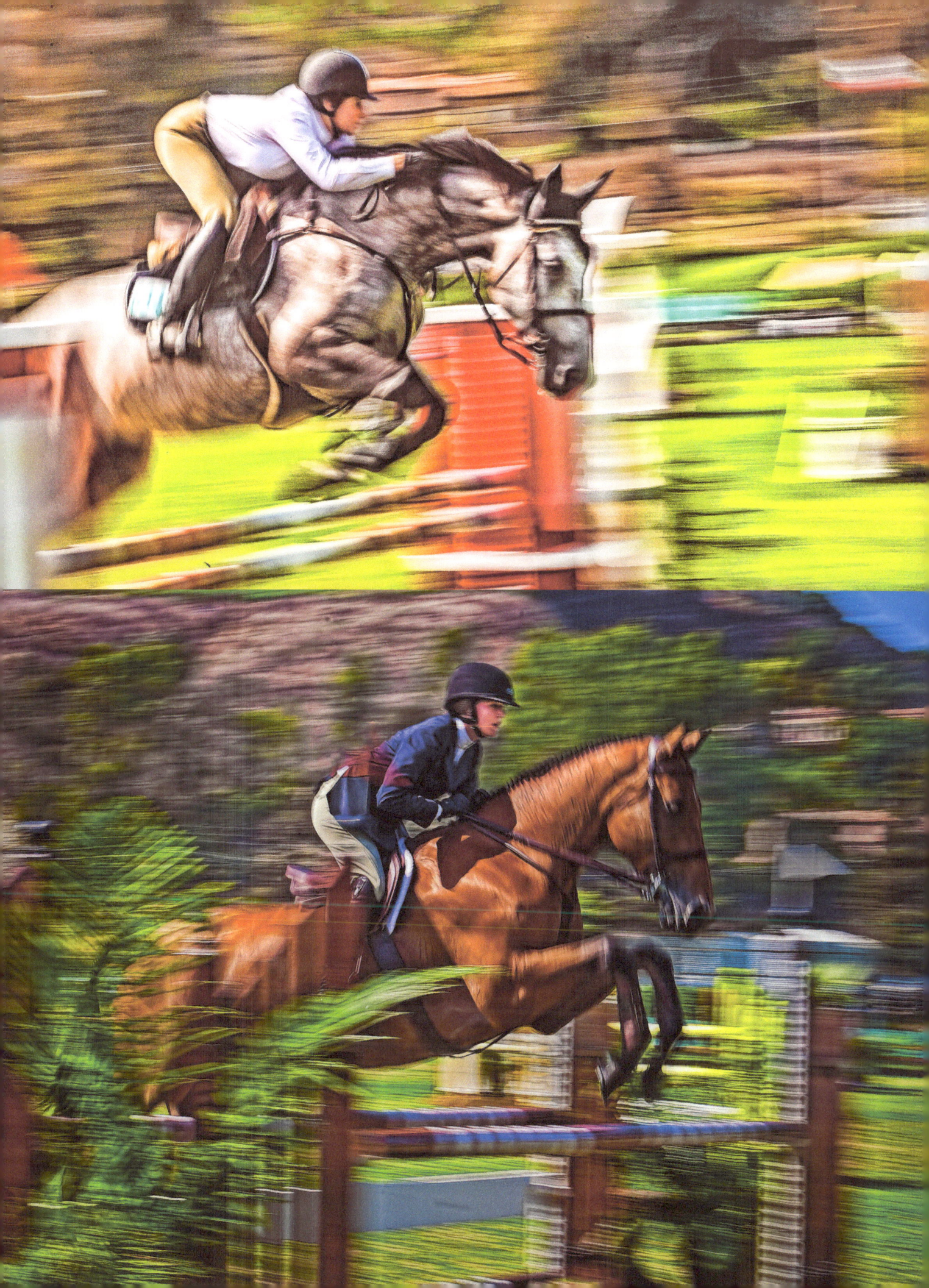

Many of the action shots taken in our day and age do not fit into any one of the four categories mentioned. Chances are they are unintentional hybrids of two or more of the methods. It is also probable that a huge percentage of the most creative action shots have come about as accidents.

Embrace your fortunate mishaps. Important photographers with a reputation to uphold may feel they have to come up with a long winded explanation of how the shot was planned and constructed, but you don't have to. Remember, ultimately, it is the results that count. No one is going to worry about how you got yours. If you are asked, just tell the truth.

If you are happy with your results, everything is fine. If you are not, change something in your strategy. If that gets you where you want to be, fine. If not, make another change, and so on and so forth!

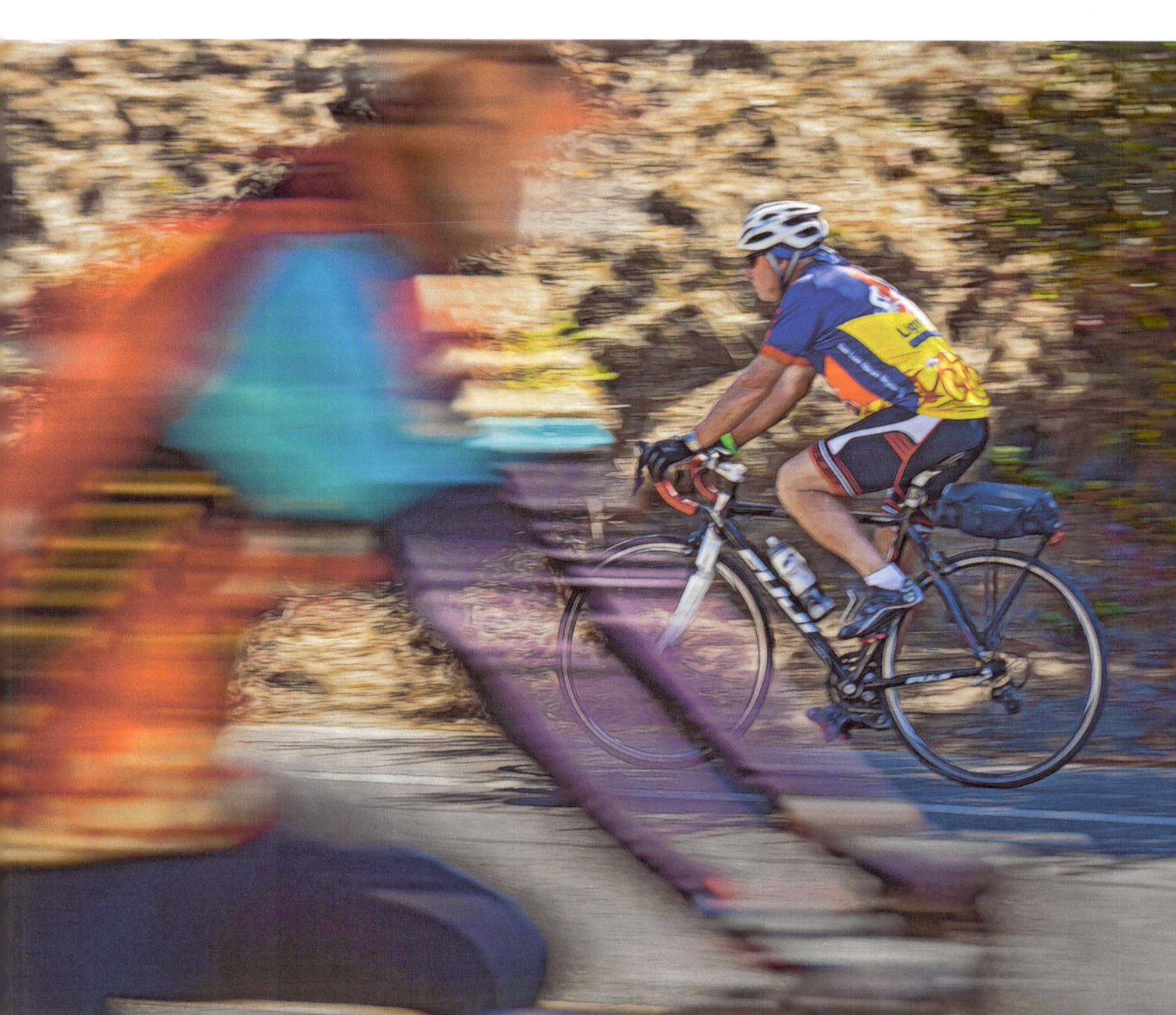

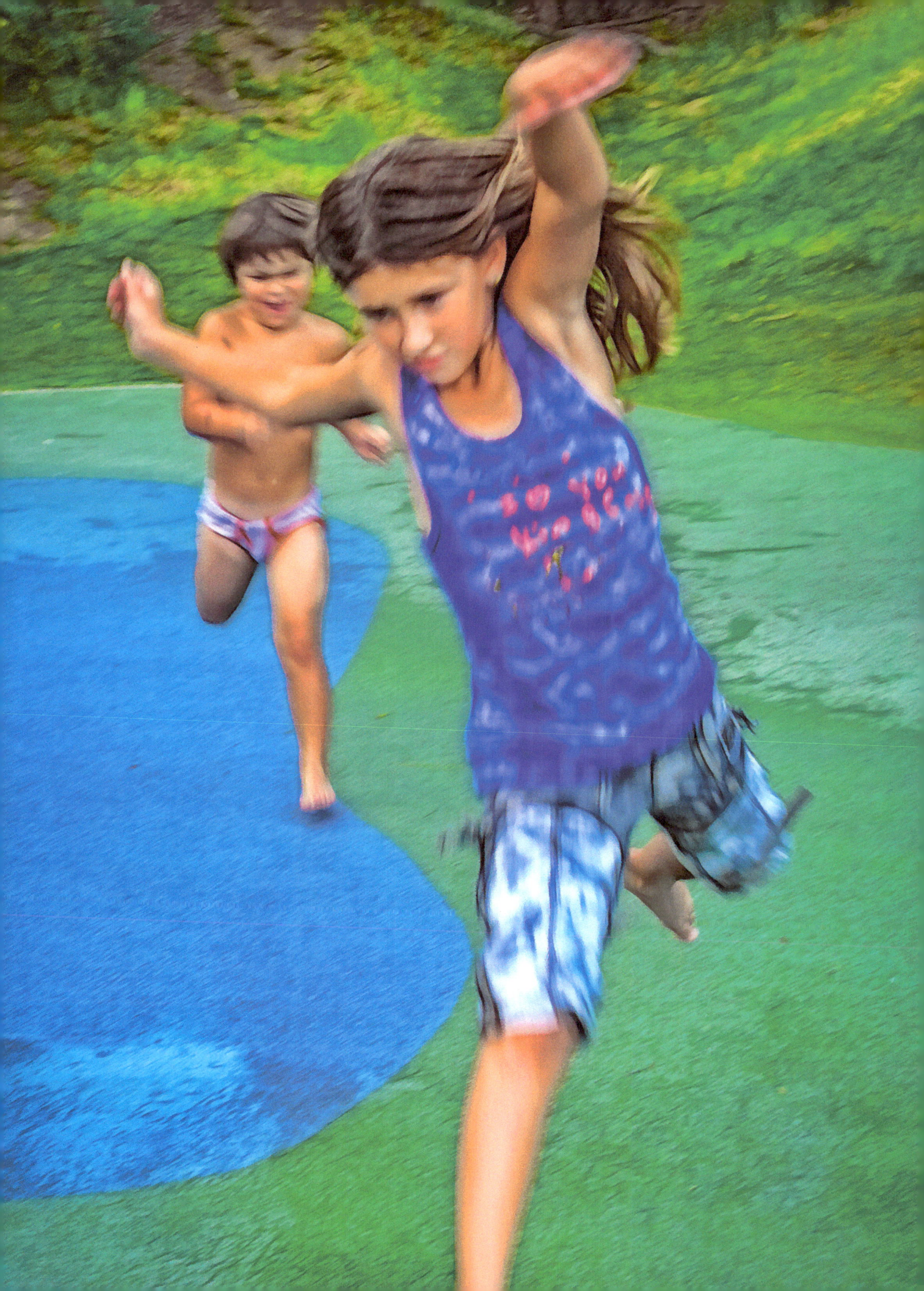

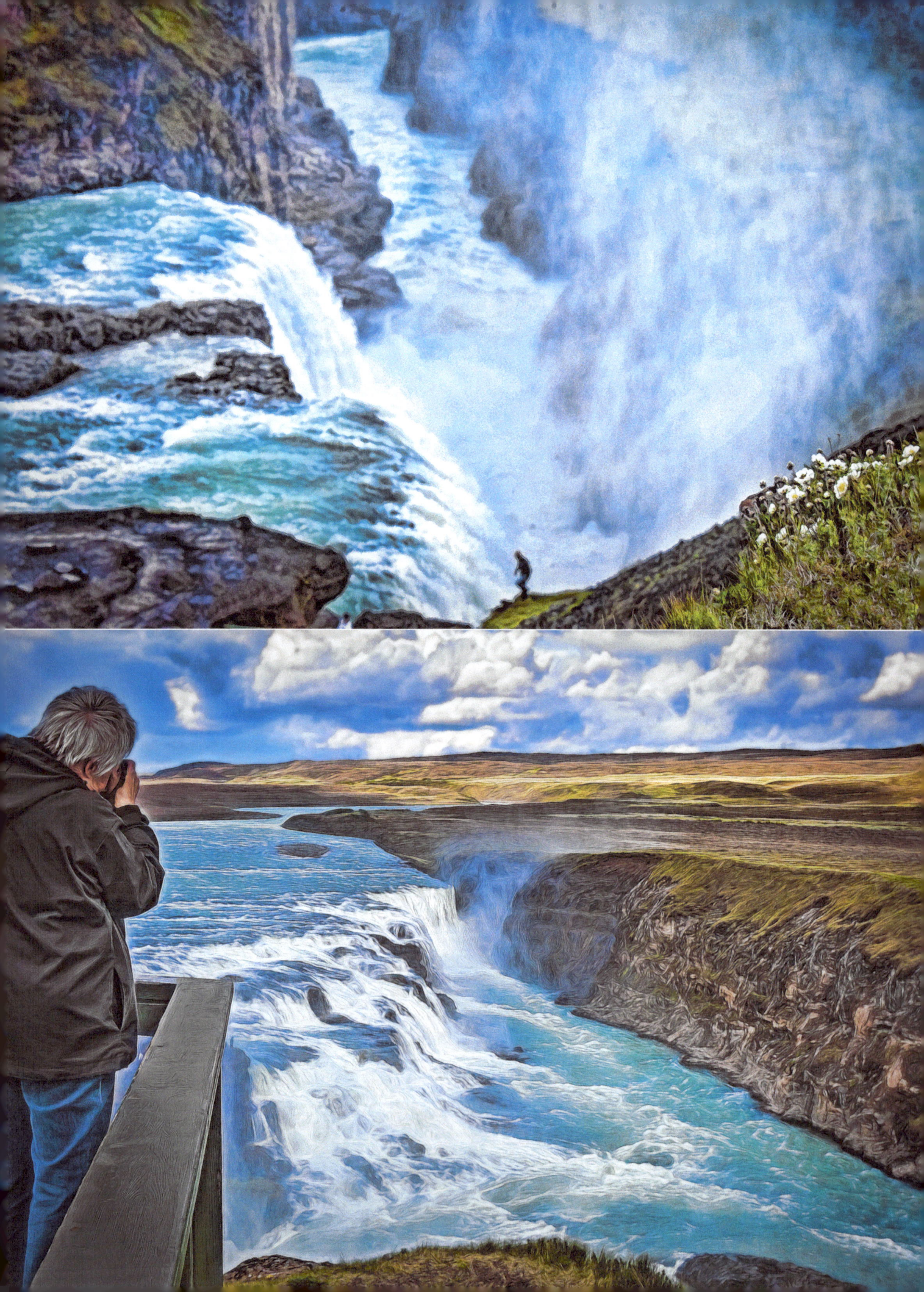

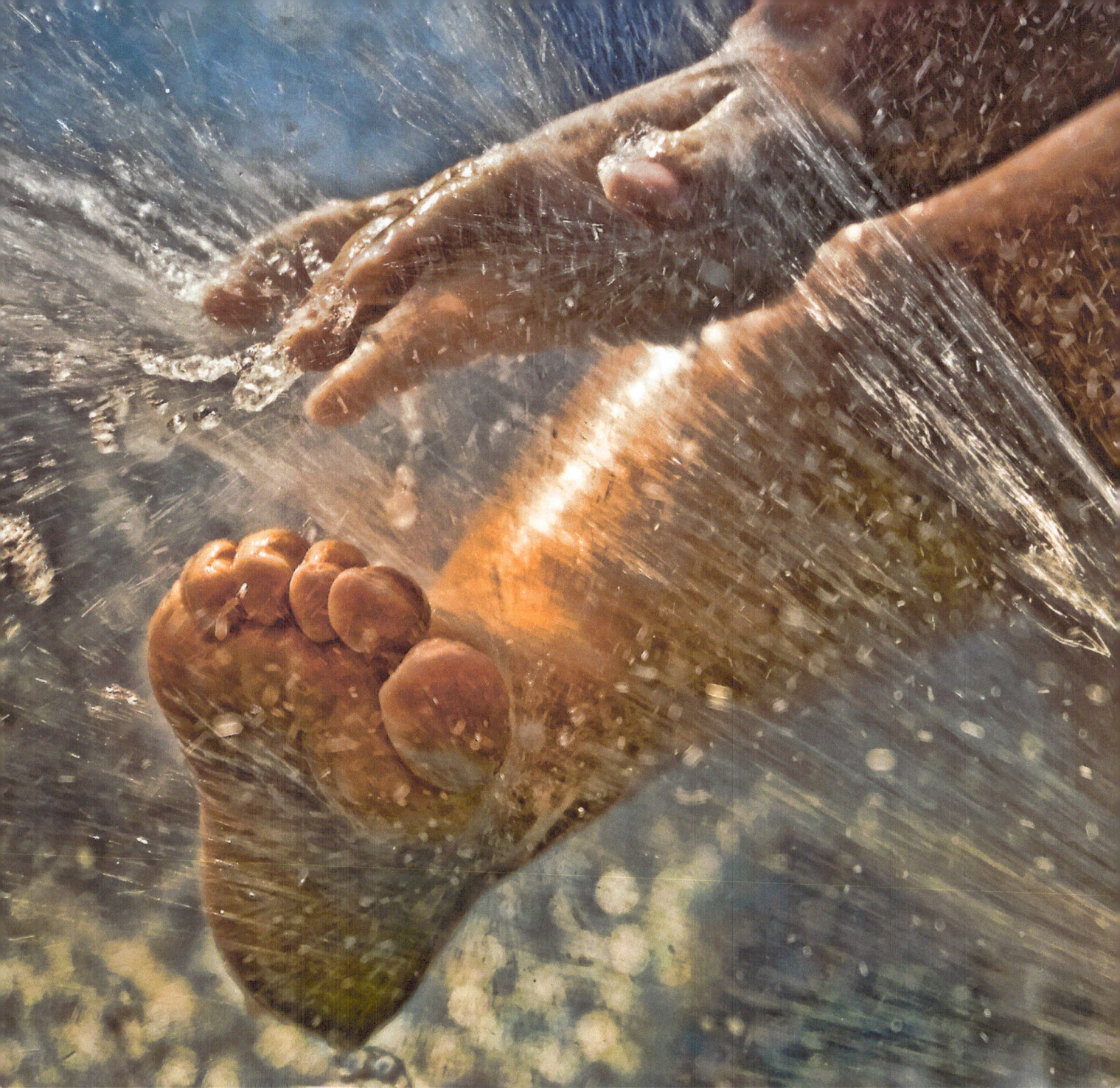

Add power to your photography. Embrace the forces of nature!

The photos to the left are from the famous waterfall, Gullfoss, in Iceland. My aim here was to show the grandiosity of the scenery and the power of the raging water. I included people in the scenes in an effort to show dimension and to create a feeling of connection to the viewer.

The photo above is taken in a water park To me the close-up on the hand and foot are an "in your face" type of powerful. Even without seeing the face of the child, I feel we can sense his or her joy in the moment.

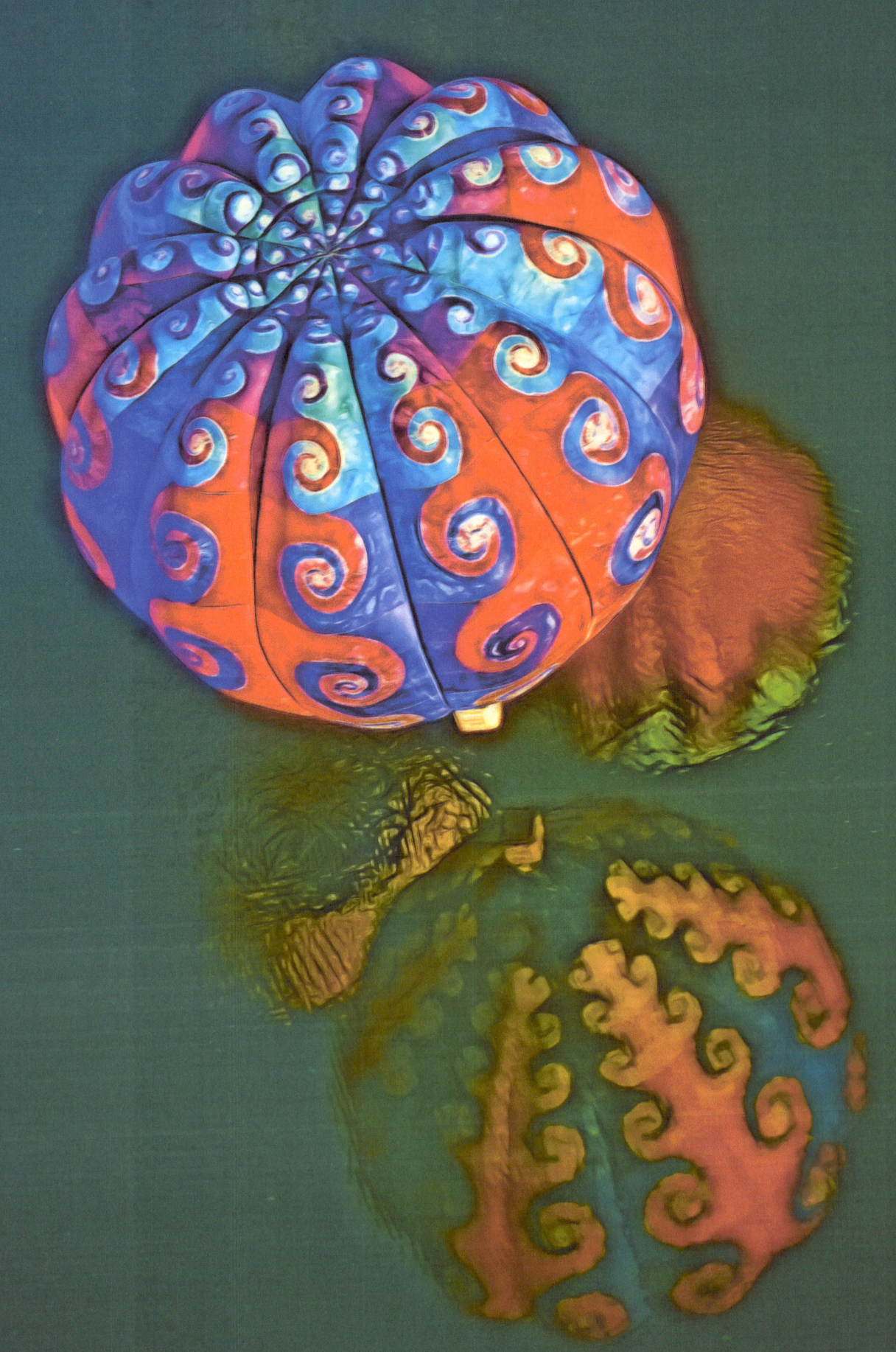

Soar with the eagles, oops, balloons!

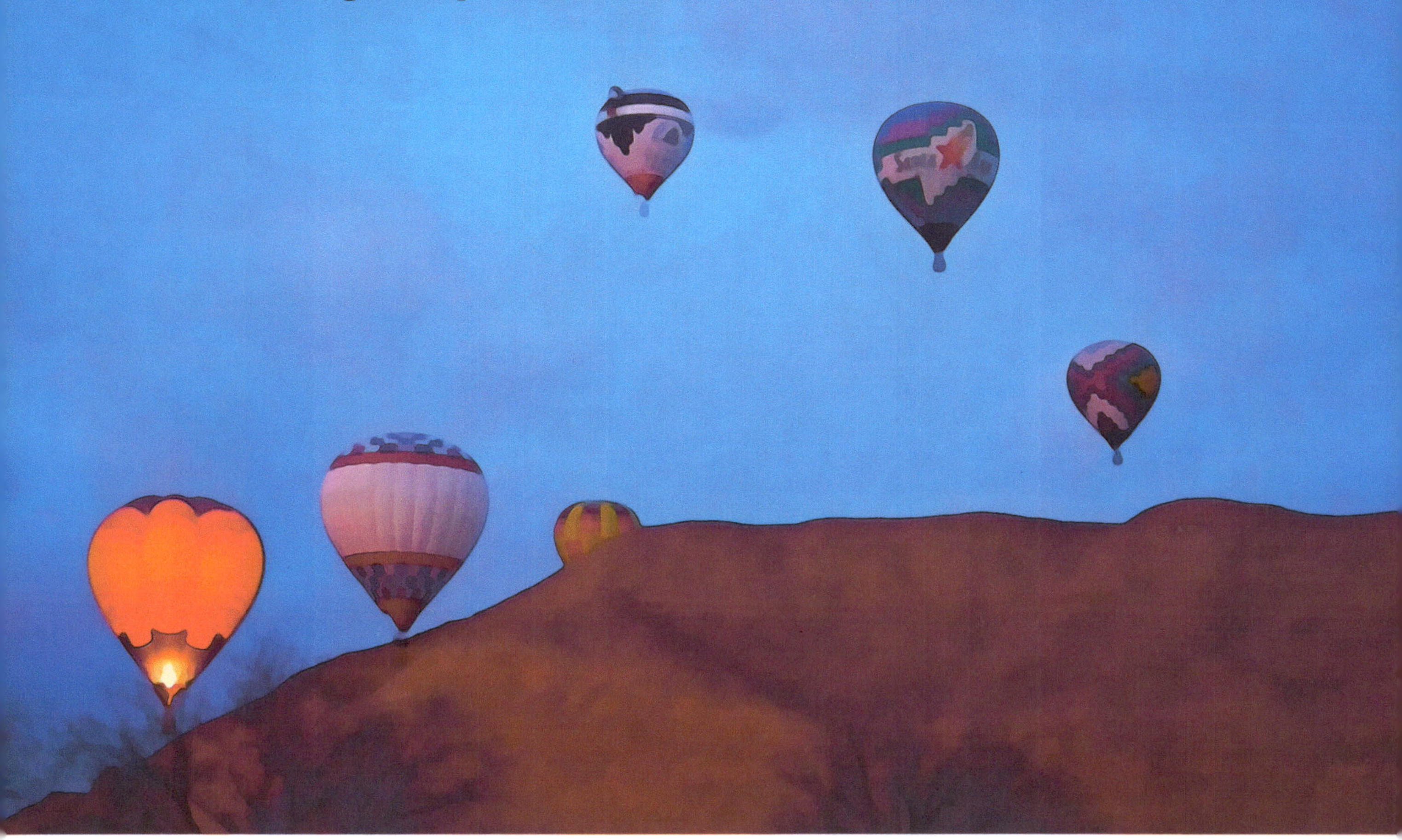

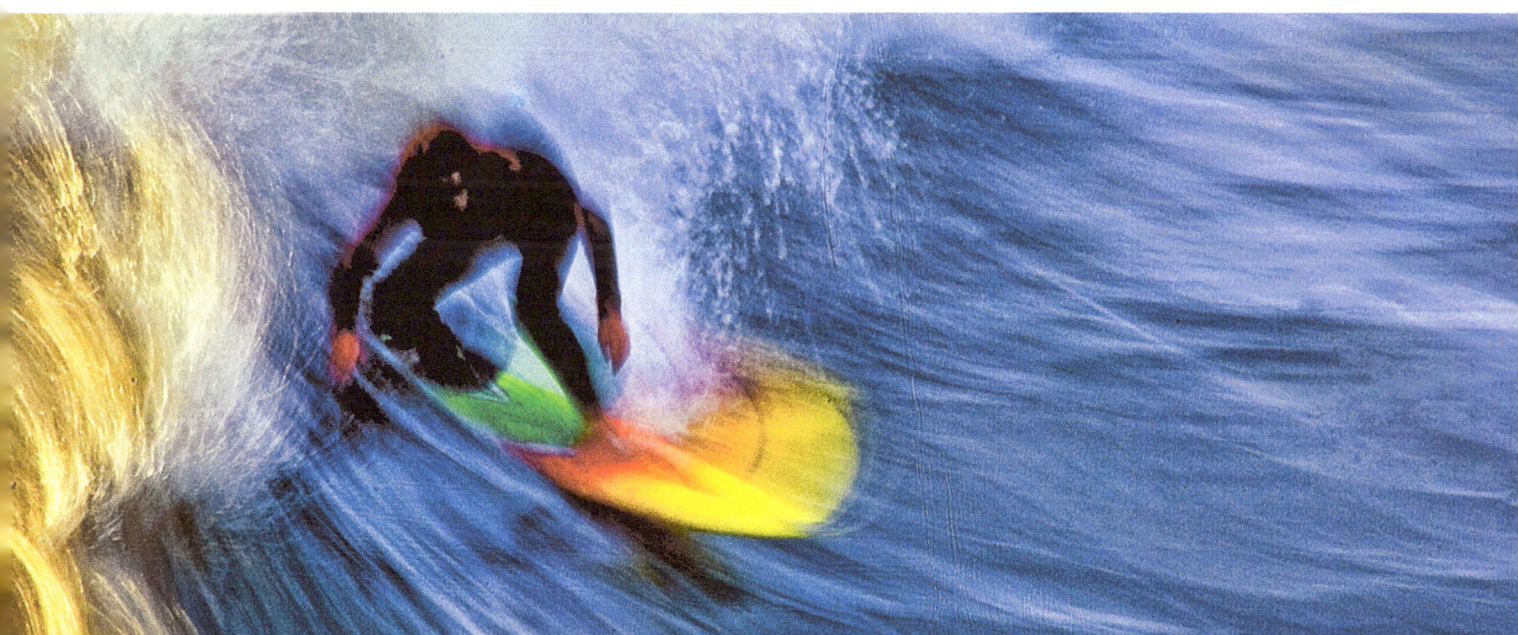

Balloons are fun and rewarding to photograph. Practically everyone is in love with them. They are fun, colorful, and exciting. They set our imagination in motion, make us dream of soaring, and of going to far away places.

Just looking at the photos, we may not associate balloons with fast movement, but when in the air and caught by the breeze, they travel faster than surfers normally do. Nonetheless,they are reasonably easy to shoot. The secret is composition—to get all the ducks—oops, balloons in a row.

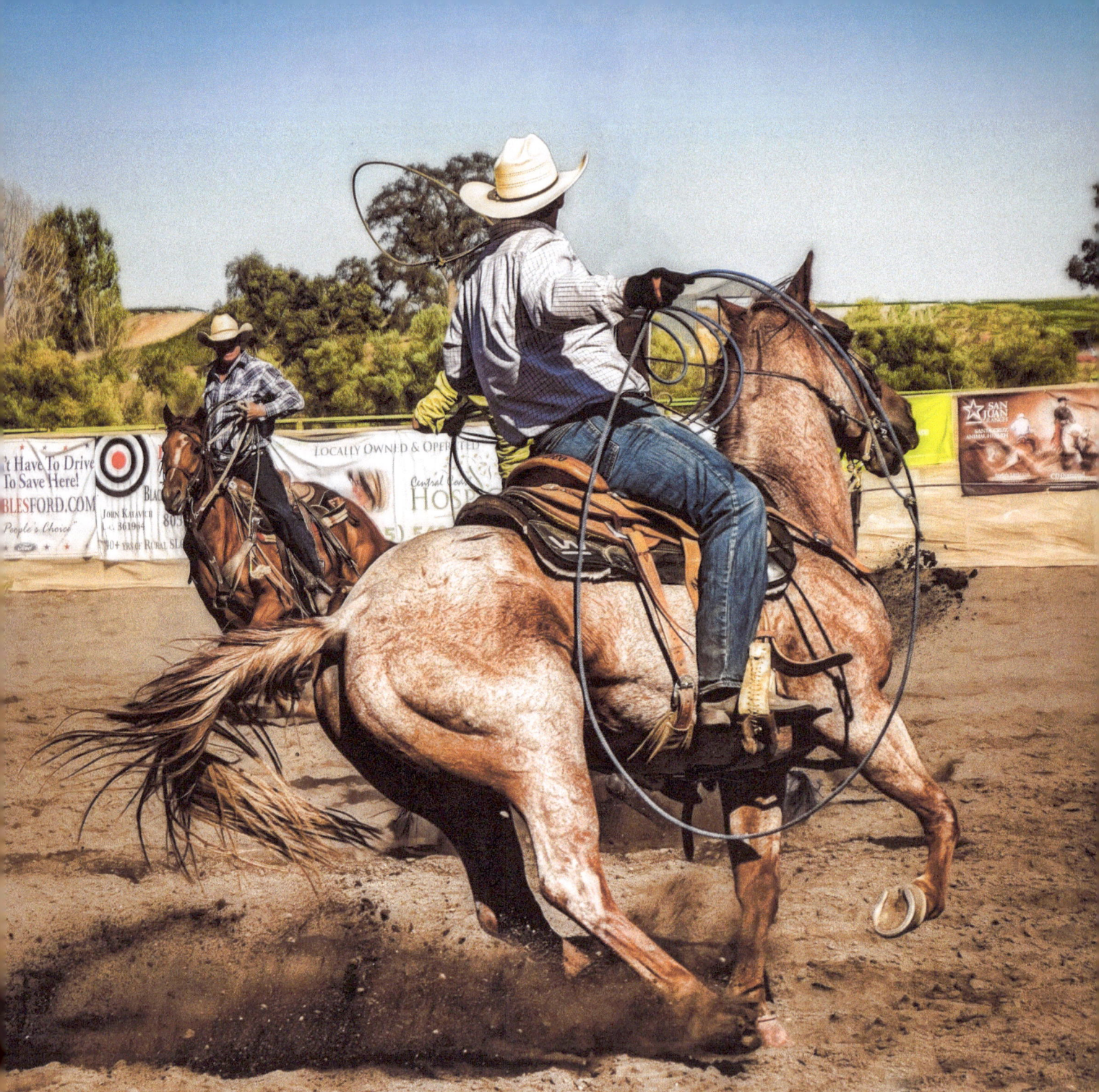

Somewhere, at some point, someone coined a phrase about capturing the moment. Somehow the catch phrase stuck. The idea is absurd, of course. Moments are fleeting. They don't wait for anyone. They are here one split second and gone the next.

Nonetheless, moments can be commemorated provided you are prepared, alert, and fast on the draw. Remember the importance of engaging your shutter at the peak moment or just before it. Balance is important in the composition of the photo as well as in the subject.

Be proactive rather than reactive!

Focus a tad in front of the action and allow it to catch up to you. Take lag time into account. Allow for the split second delay between when you decide to focus and when you actually fire. Each camera and lens combination has a different lag time. Become aware of your parameters. Make taking them into account automatic and incorporate the results in your muscle memory.

The action is frozen in each of the photos in this spread. They were taken at a recent local rodeo here on the California Central Coast.

Whereas the balance of all the horses in these shots is impressive what really makes these shots stand out is the determination, direction, and balance of the rider below, and the synchronicity between the two horse and rider combinations on the photo to the left.

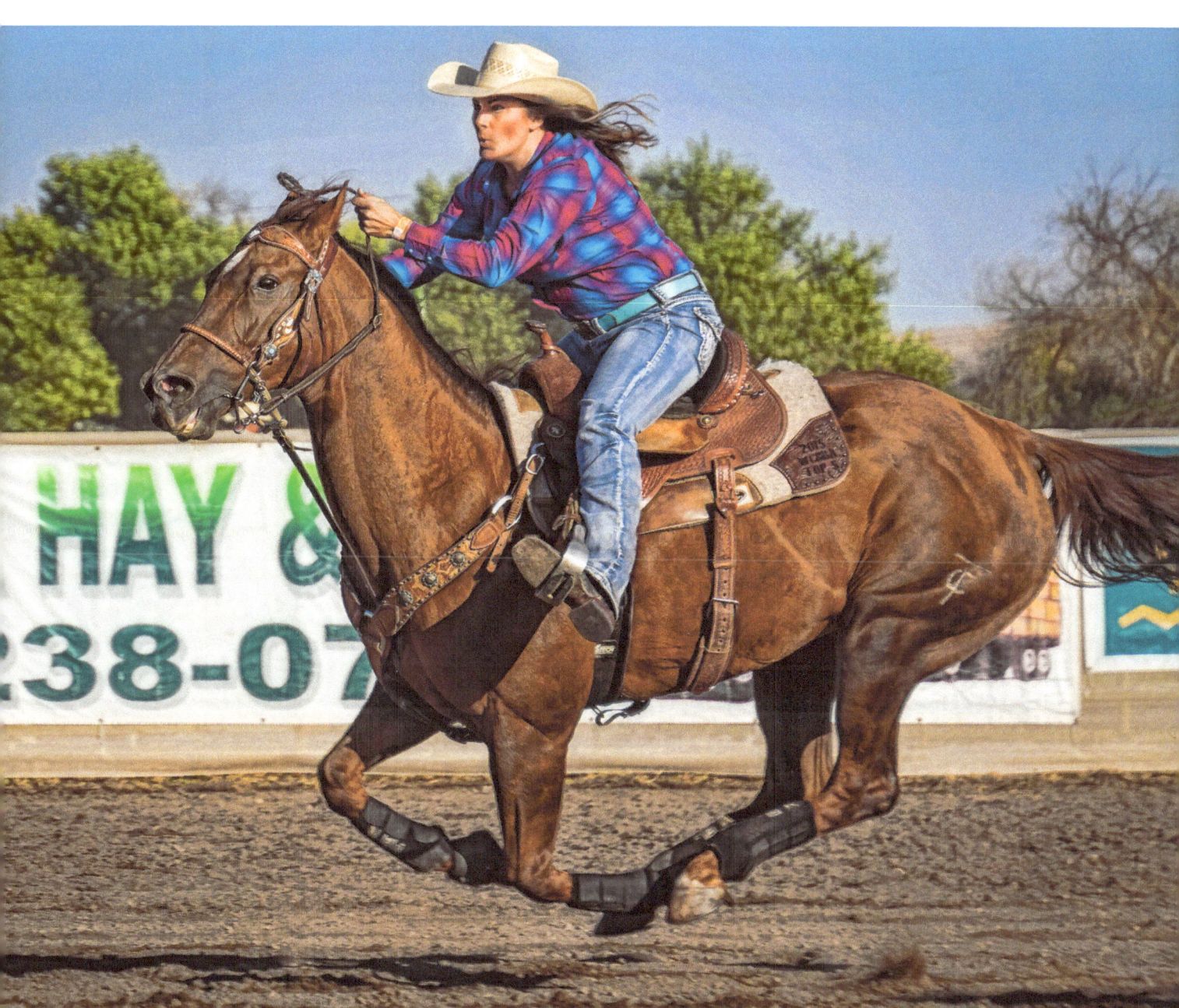

Photographing groups (patterns) is one of the most challenging facets of photography—especially when the subjects are moving. Groups are also one of the most attention getting, emotion triggering, and rewarding subjects.

Other than the usual, some of the most important things to take into consideration when photographing groups are:

- Look for strong, pleasing leading lines (cookie crumb trails).
- It is important to establish connection between the individuals in the pattern, but it almost as important to establish separation. Allow space between components. Avoid one great, big jumble!
- As much as possible, avoid individual subjects practically covering each other. It is especially important to not have one member covering the head of another.
- Unless the group is moving towards a goal where we would like to follow it, photograph the group coming towards you, in either front or side view.
- Look for synchronicity in movement, color, and type.
- Including one unique (different from the others) element in a group attracts attention and stirs emotion.

Be inspired by others and what they create, but add your own twist!

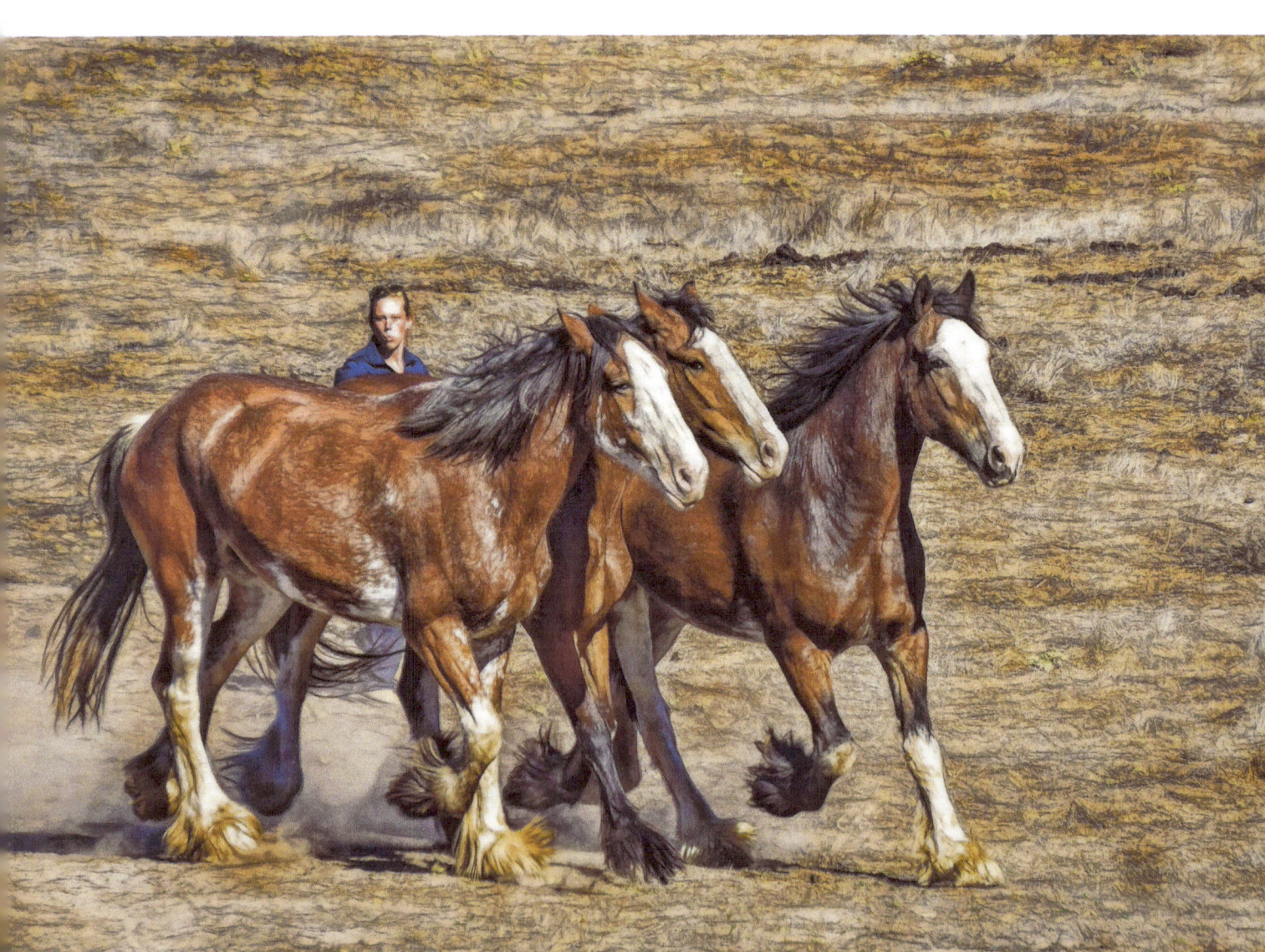

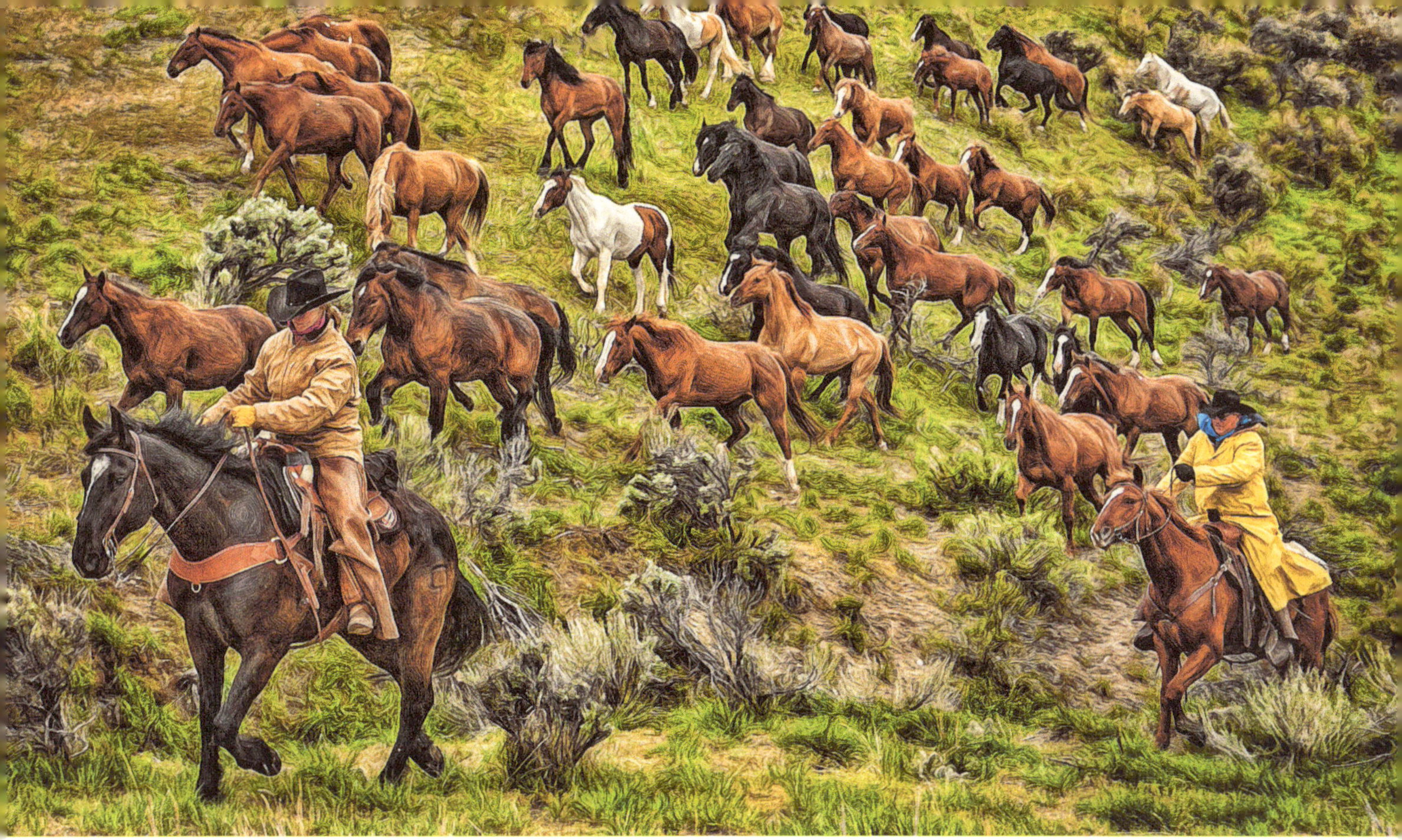

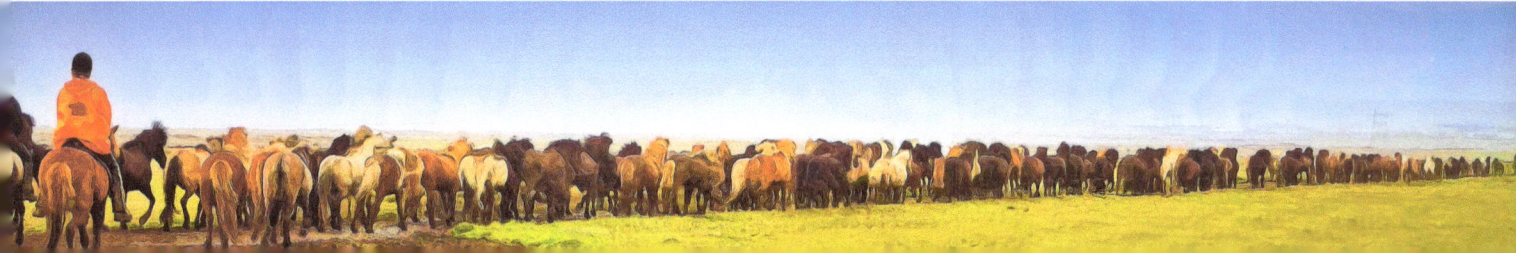

Horses stir human emotions. They are symbols of so many concepts: Freedom, power, speed, pride, nobility, beauty, and gentleness. As a result they make great photo models—especially when they are running free in a herd.

The photo on the left hand side of the spread is from a Clydesdale ranch in Cambria where I live on the California Central Coast. A large herd of horses freely roam the hills of a large ranch. The large animals are impressive and fun to photograph. Notice the synchronicity. All three giants are in exactly the same phase of their trot. That, their color, and their blazes all create a connection between the horses. Although the horses partly cover each other, their heads are free. The blurred girl in the background of the photo adds a dash of "dare to be different element" to the photo.

The photo above is from a huge horse drive in Colorado. Notice the strong leading lines and the movement synchronicity between the two horses in the foreground. Whereas a few of the horses almost cover one another, you still get a sense of the individuals.

The photo below is from Iceland where traveling with horses is still common. The horses are moving away from us. Normally that is a negative. The reason it works in this case is that we can see the whole moving herd and feel as if we are, traveling with the group as a part of it.

Expect the unexpected!

Because there are so many last minute things to worry about when shooting action, it is prudent to develop a practical work flow.

Be prepared! Check your camera settings before you leave home, and choose a combination that will serve you in most situations.

Realize that making action photography your favorite genre does not limit you to motion, only. When it comes to photography, I am like a chicken who instinctively takes a bite of every new food thrown in front of it regardless of it being full. I automatically focus on and shoot everything that catches my eye regardless of genre.

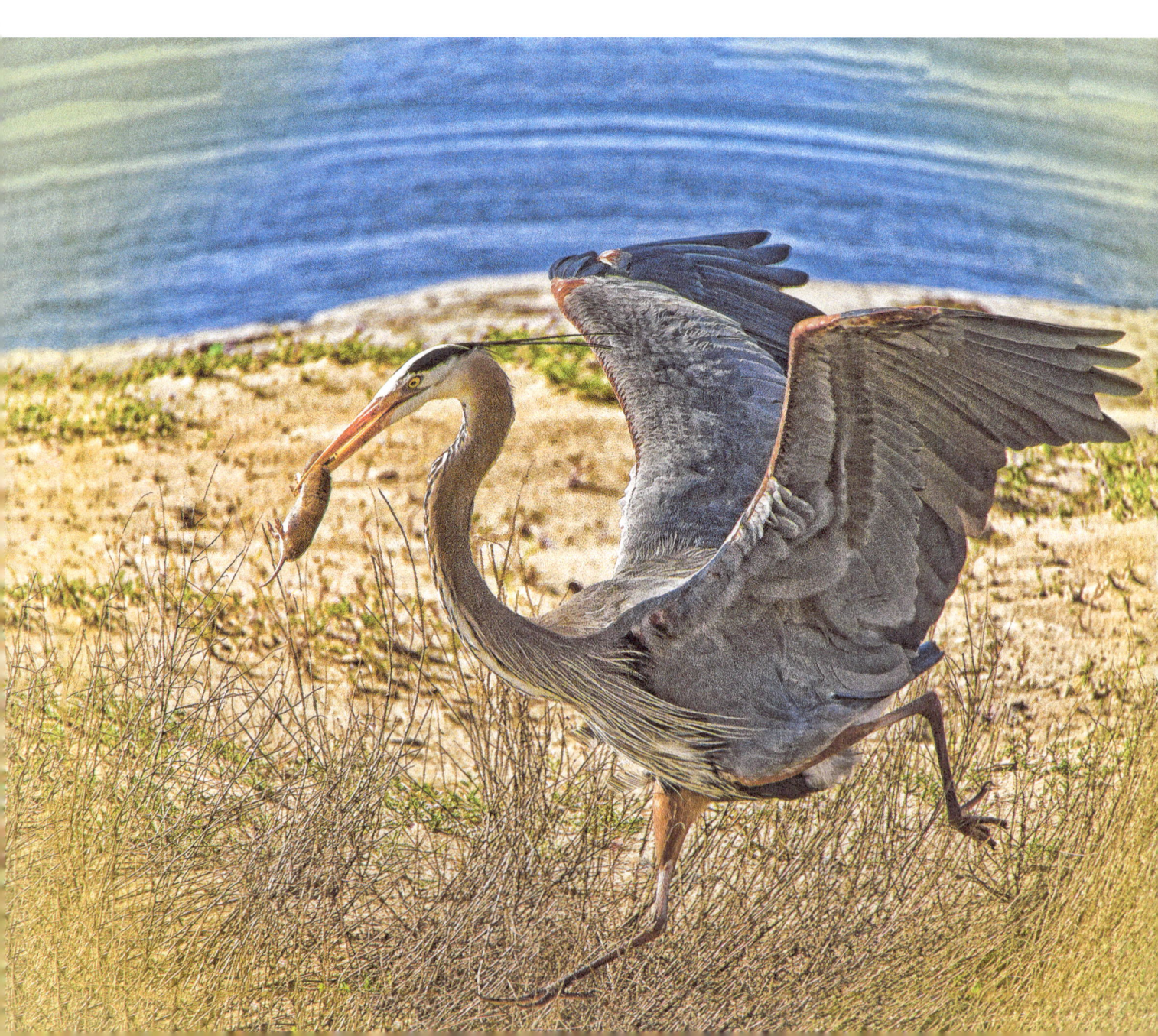

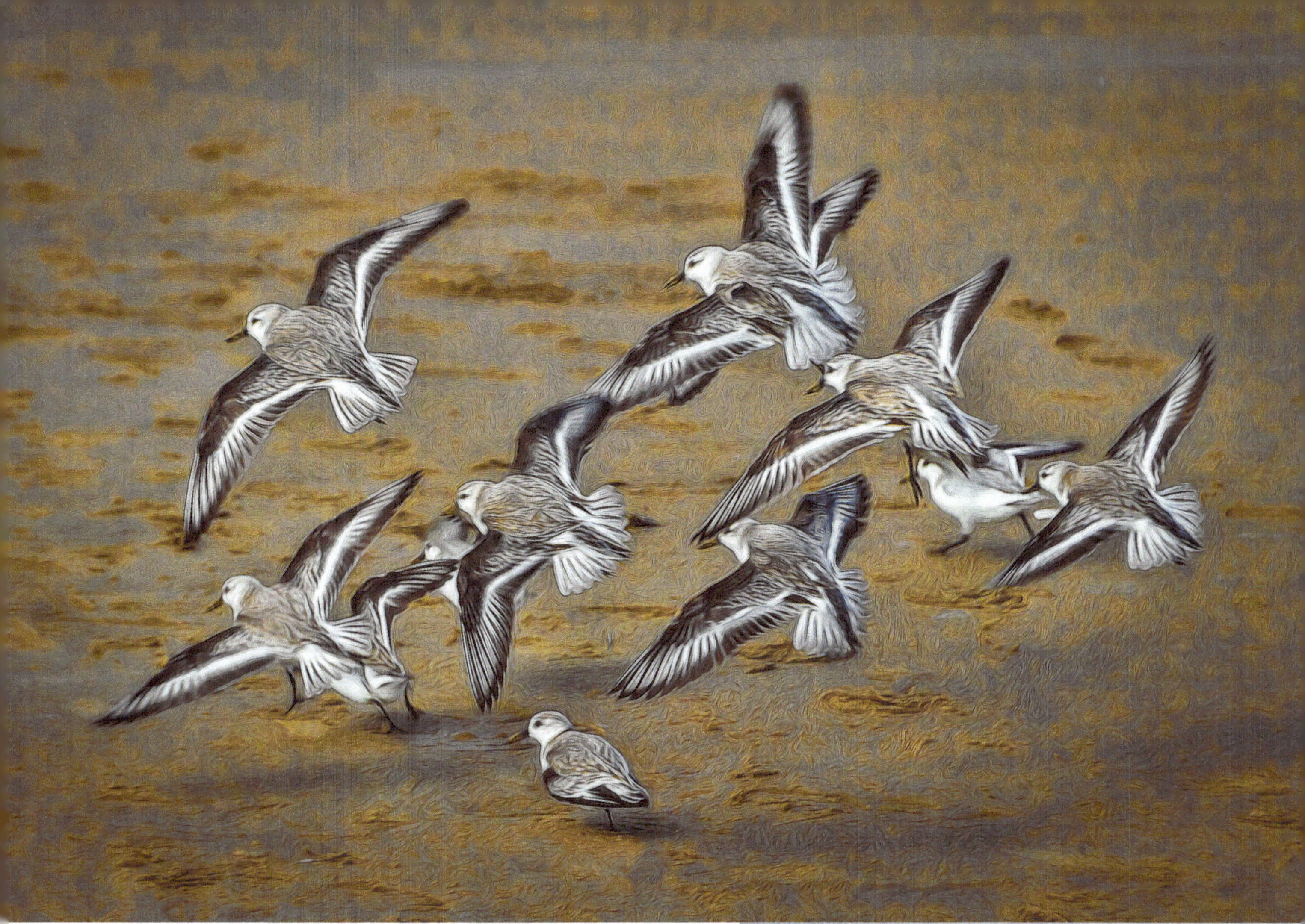

Learn to soar. Let go of more ego and acquire more humility.

Realize that every action is a dance and has a flow—a sequence of steps—that once begun—always follow one another. Once the sequence is completed, it is usually repeated verbatim.

- Cars stop, go, and turn.
- Bicycles travel in a straight line, and their riders keep their balance, and pedal.
- Ducks waddle and/or fly.
- When one Sanderling takes off the rest follow. They fly away from danger.
- Pelicans fish by bomb diving into the ocean.
- Surfers ride the waves, paddling to stay in front of the waves and to be caught by them.
- Waves roll in sets.
- Balloons rise and ride on the wind.
- Airplanes speed up and take off.

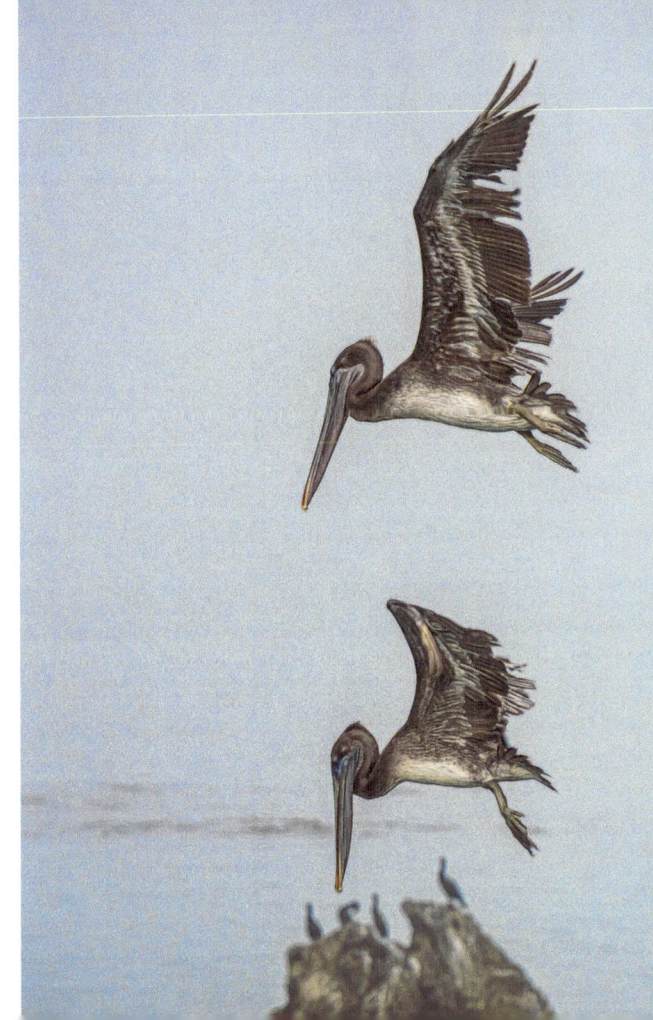

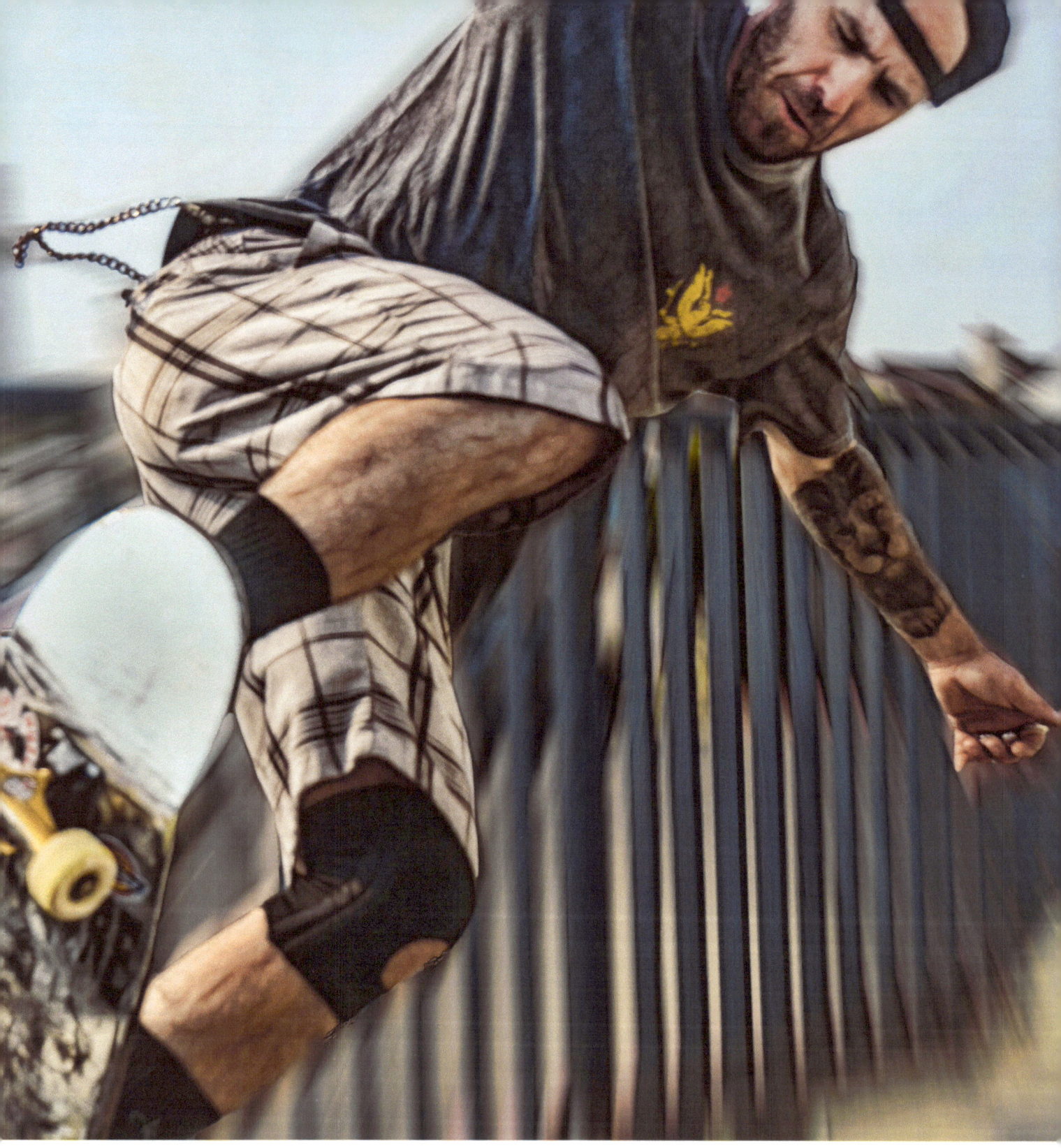

All motion is a dance. Learn to predict and anticipate its steps.

Photograph with your subconscious mind, your heart, your body, and your soul, rather than limiting yourself to using only your conscious brain!

Nowadays, most towns have public skate board parks with ramps of various slope and length. The skate boarders are fun to photograph and provide great practice.

Once you have watched the action pattern for a while, it becomes easy to predict the motion. Unfortunately the skateboarders are turned away from you quite a bit of the time. Use those shot opportunities for target practice. Just delete undesired results.

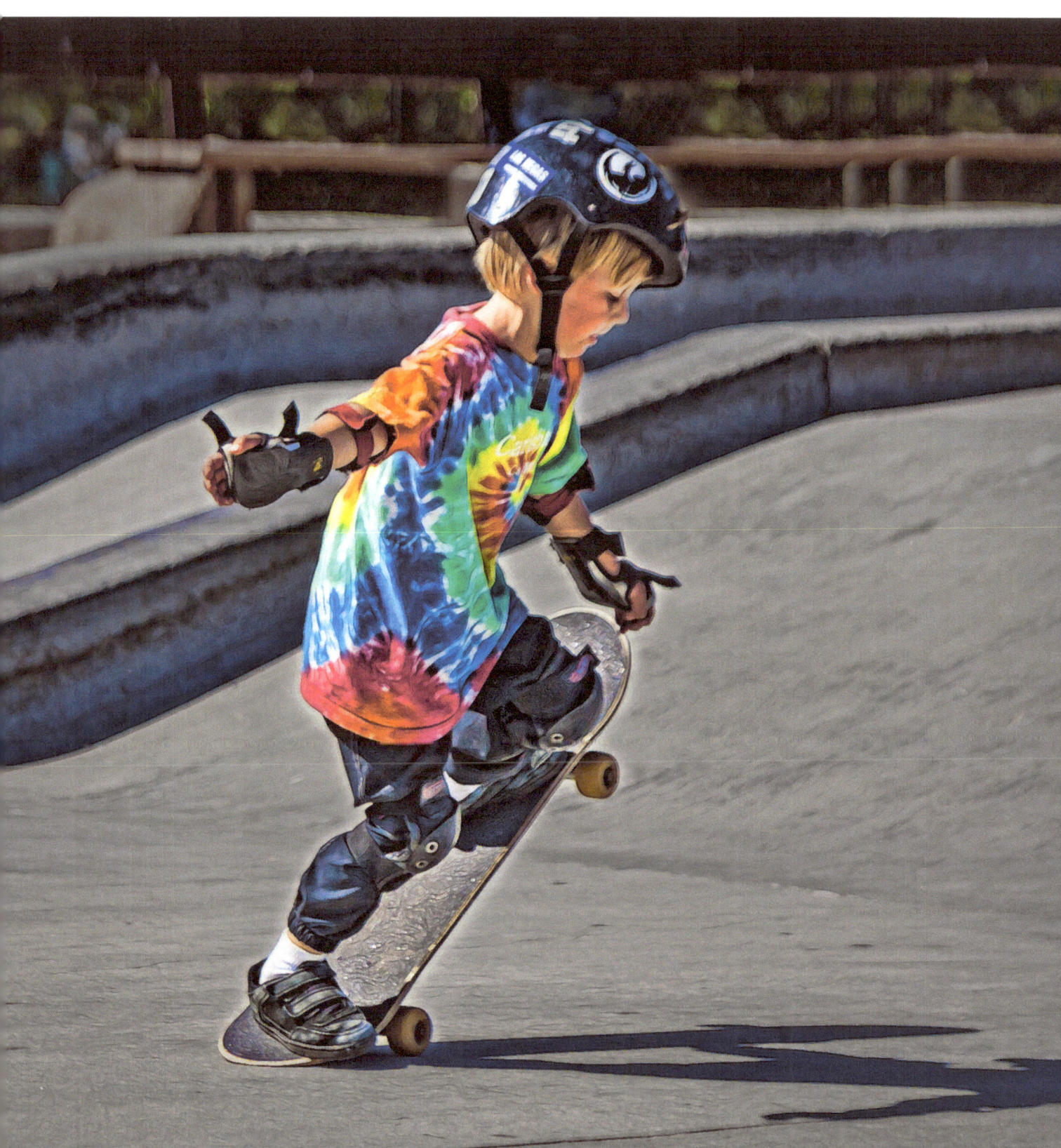

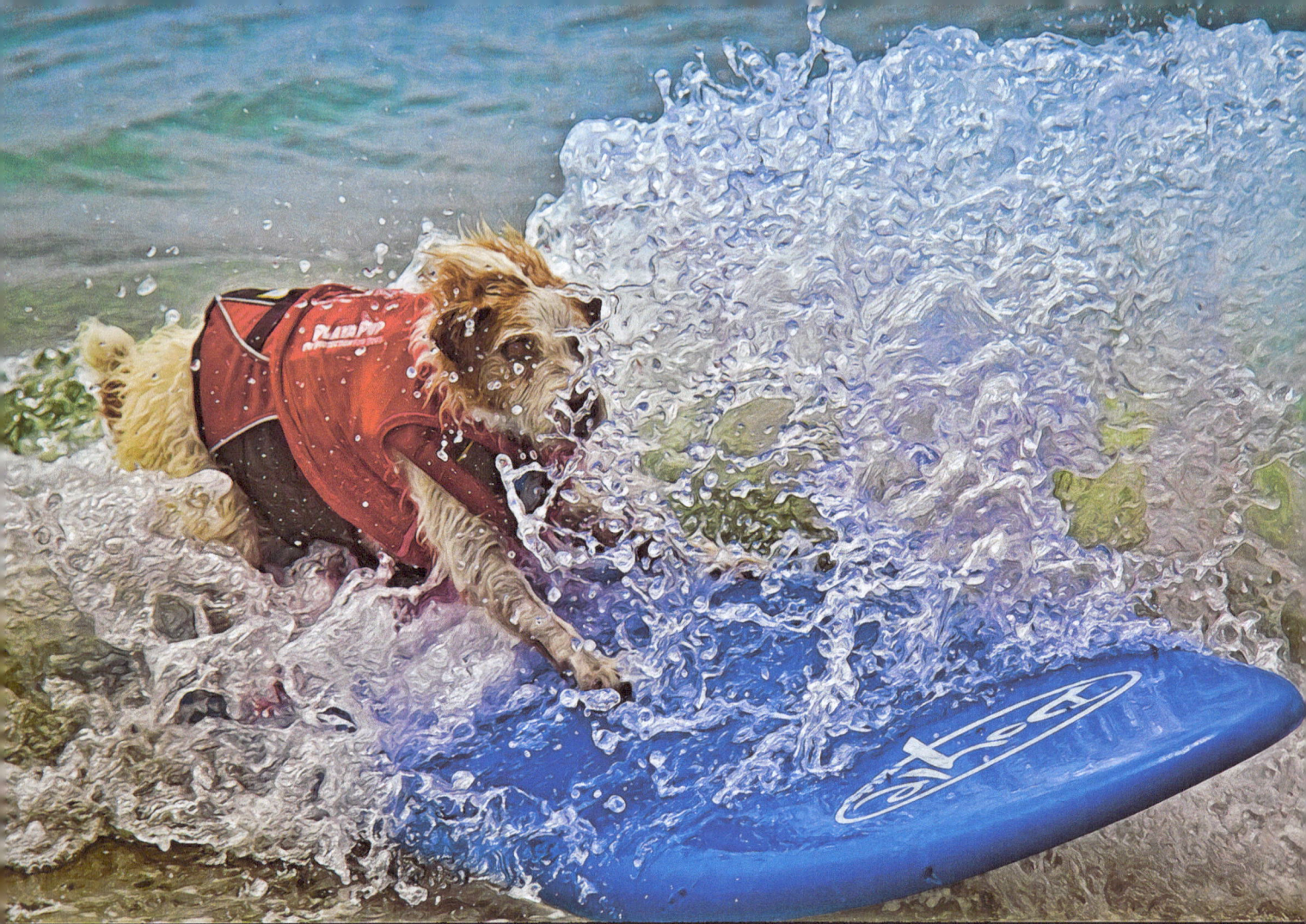

Other than the somewhat more unpredictable leaping, bucking, rearing, and spinning, four-legged animals have five foot-fall patterns they can choose from. These ways of moving are called gaits. What gait combination an individual chooses depends on its species, confirmation, and breed. Gaits are either two-beat, three-beat or four-beat.

Learning to recognize and predict the foot-fall of the individuals you are photographing is a great help when shooting animals. Some gaits are considered diagonal, meaning that a front leg moves simultaneously with the hind leg on the opposite side. Others are considered lateral, meaning that front and hind leg on the same side move at the same time. Remember all movement starts with a hind leg.

The photos on the next spread shows examples of the five gait variations, the preferred phase in which to shoot them, and the animals who favor them.

Camels, elephants, giraffes, hippos, donkeys, some dogs, and some breeds of horses are among the laterally gaited.

Cows, cats, deer, pigs, lions, zebras, buffaloes, rhinos, some dogs, and some breeds of horses are among the diagonally gaited.

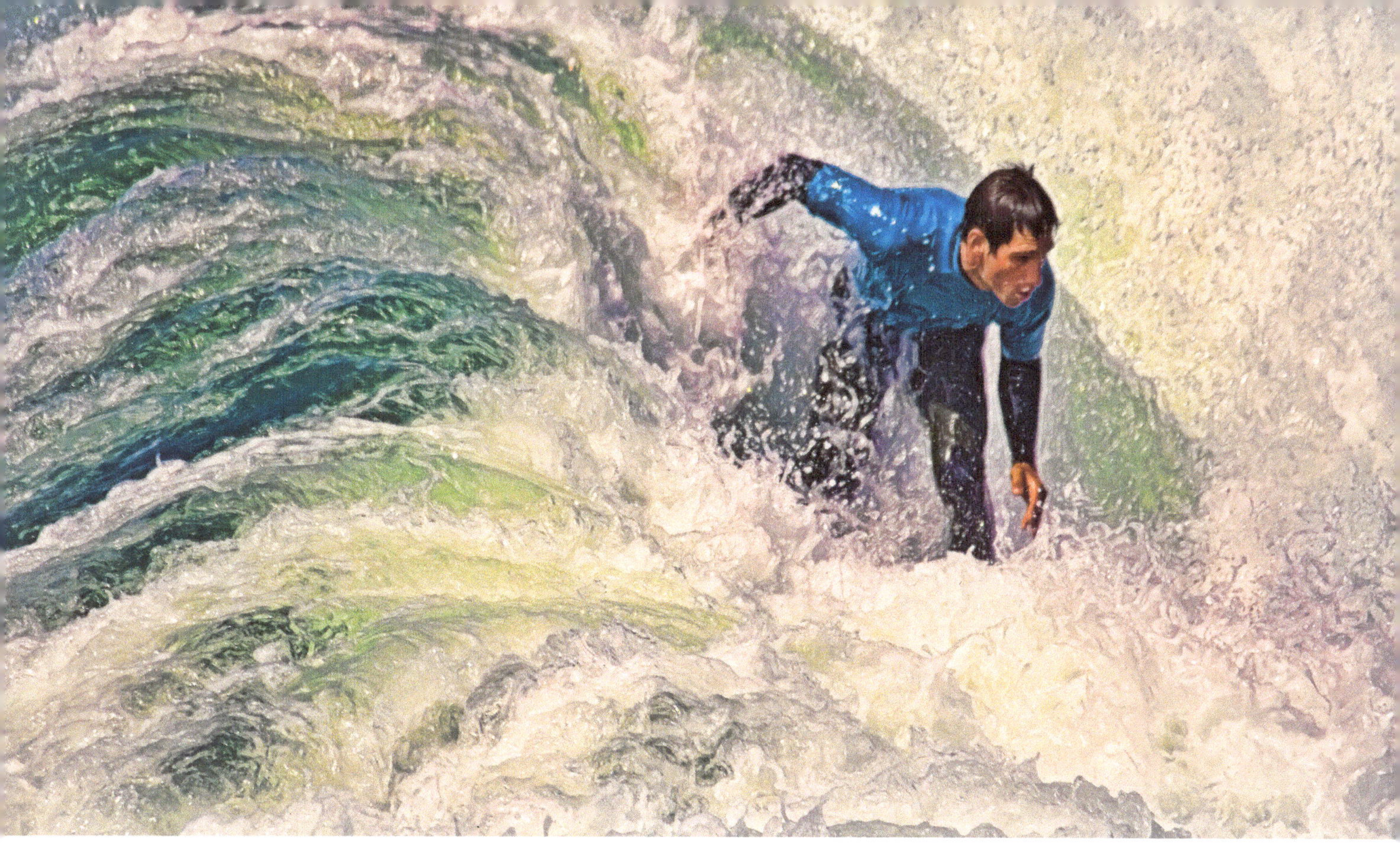

There is no gray area between pro-action and reaction!

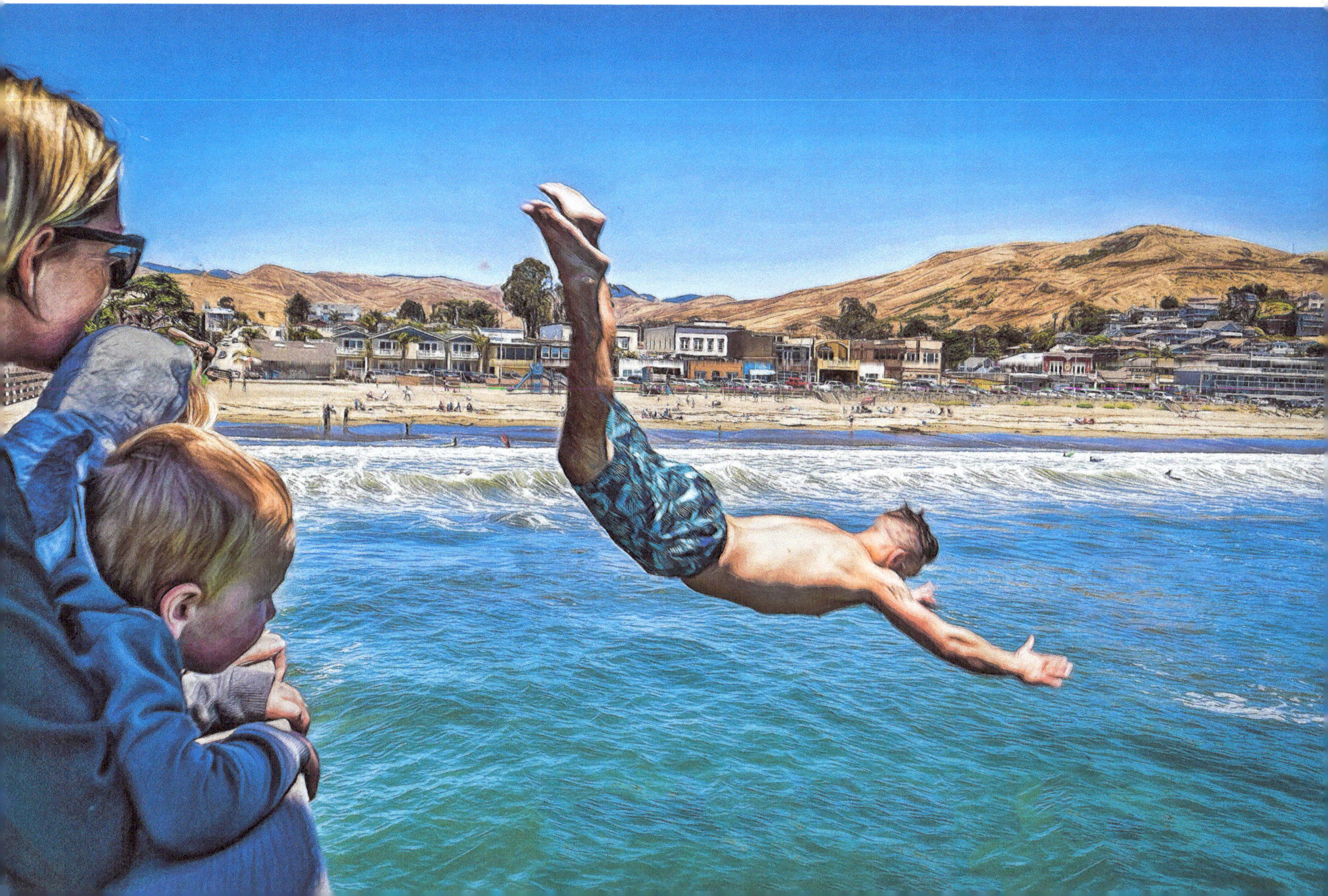

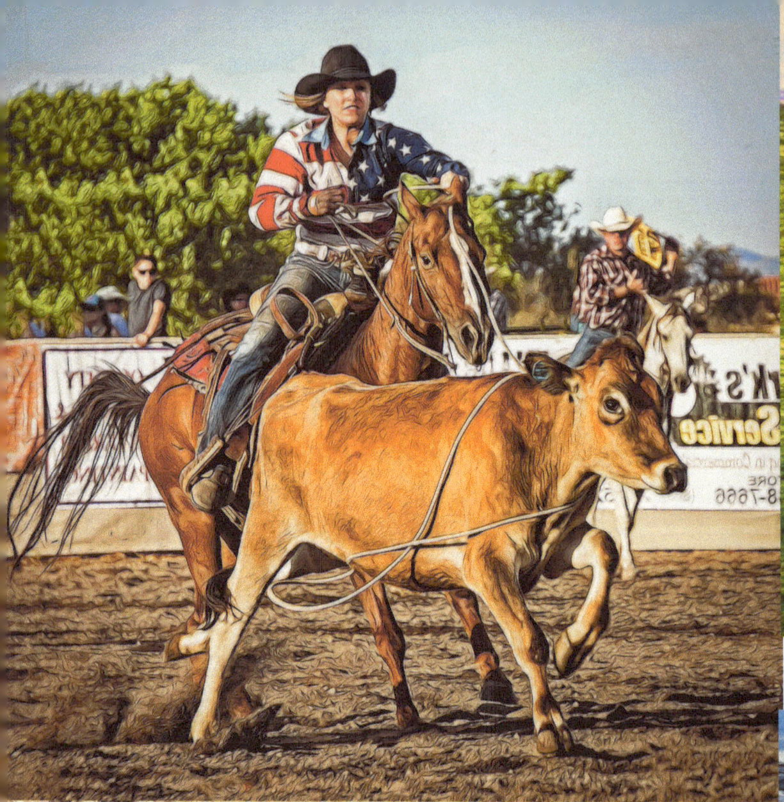

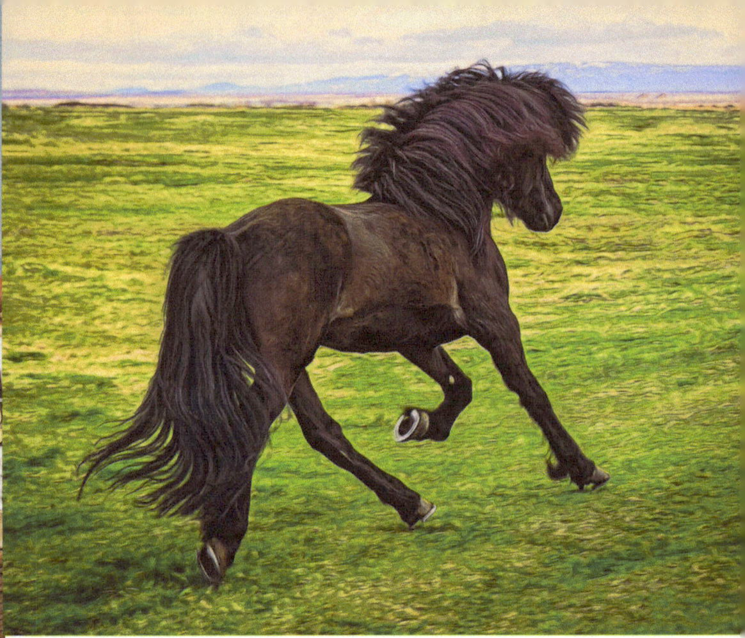

Calf to the left and black horse above both trot

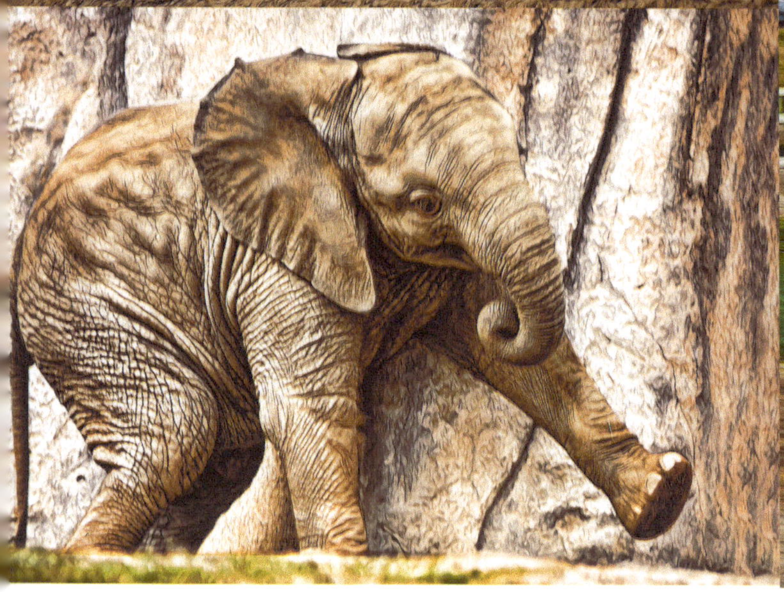

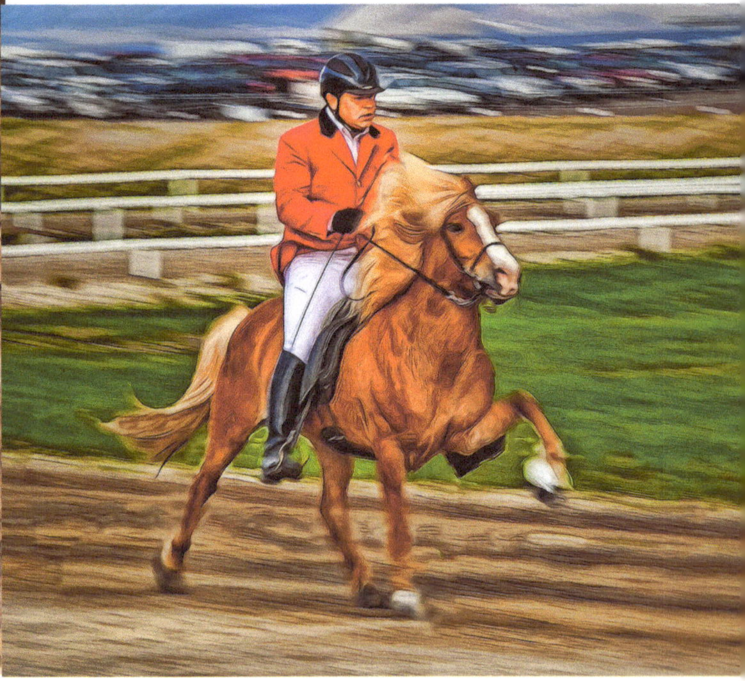

Elephant above and chestnut horse both single-foot a.k.a. toelt. Man and mule walk.

Chestnut horse and mule below both trot

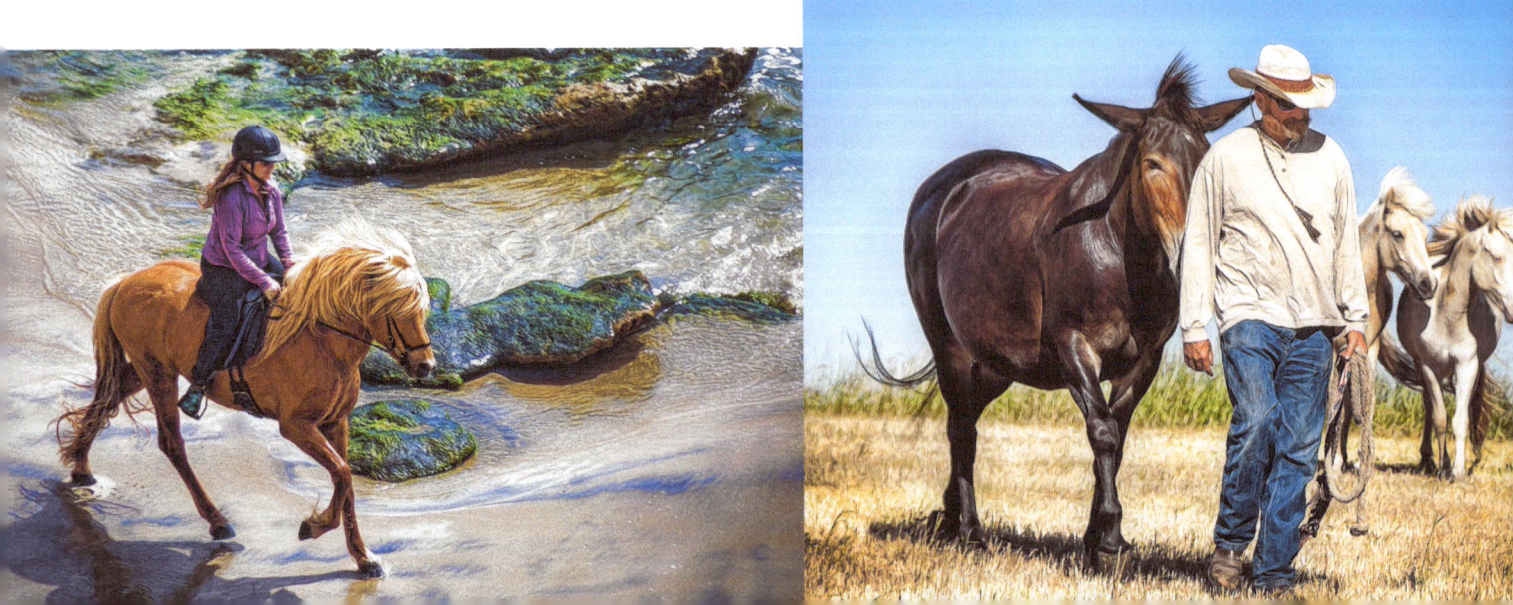

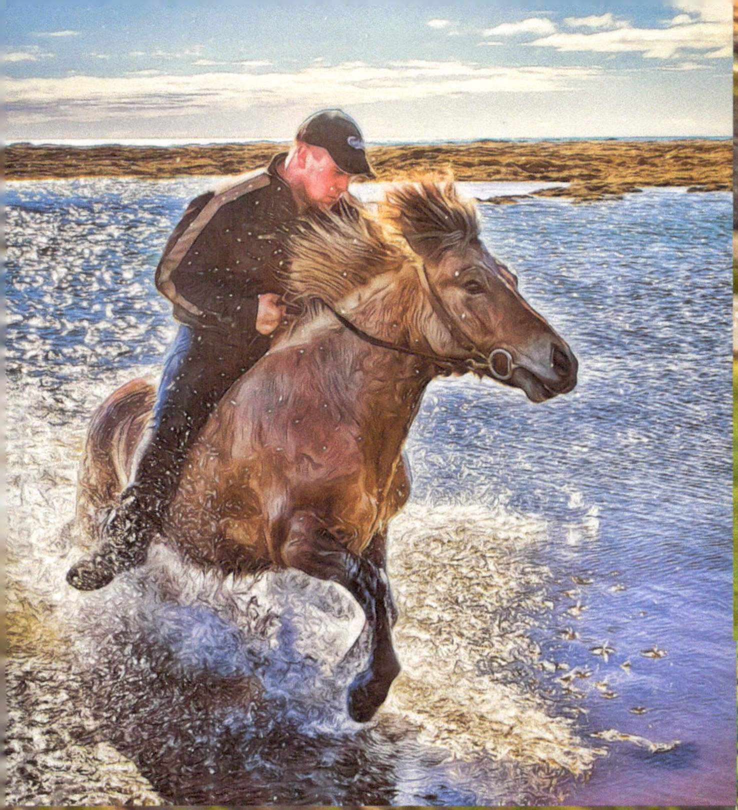

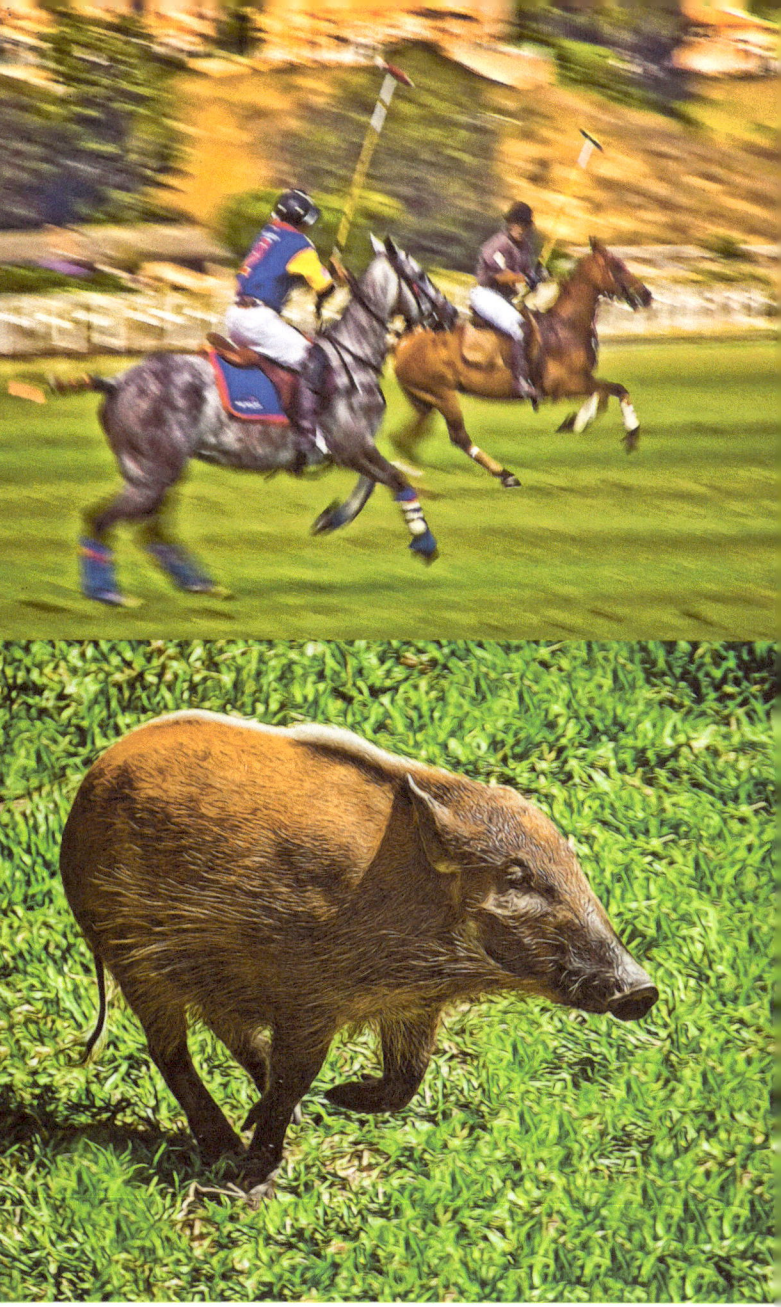

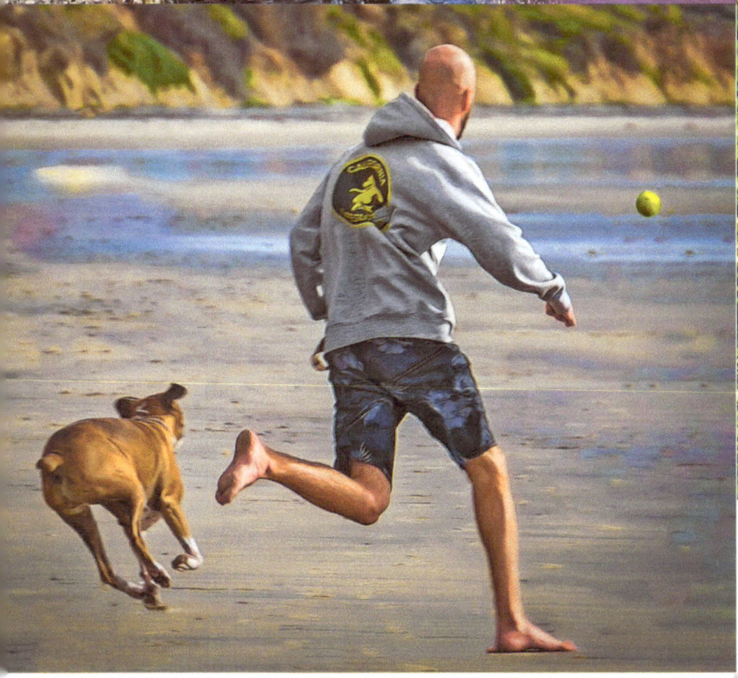

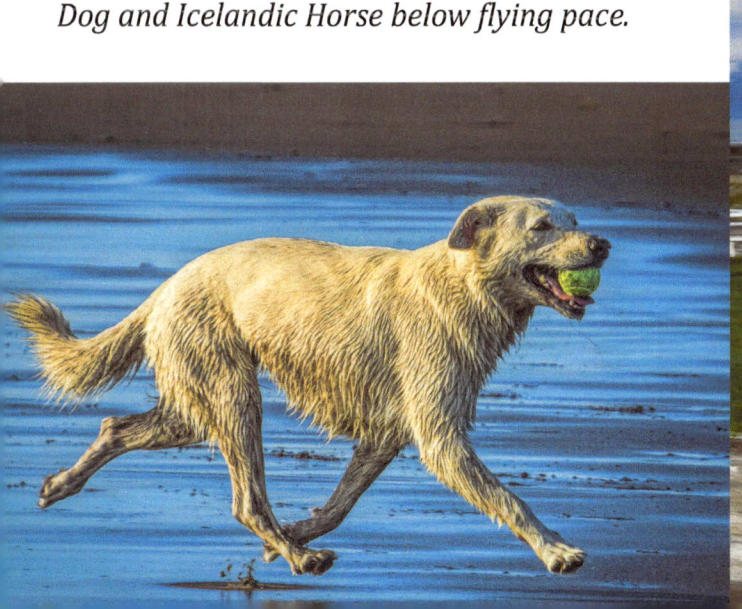

Horse in water, polo players, dog above, and pig all gallop (canter). The man is running.

Dog and Icelandic Horse below flying pace.

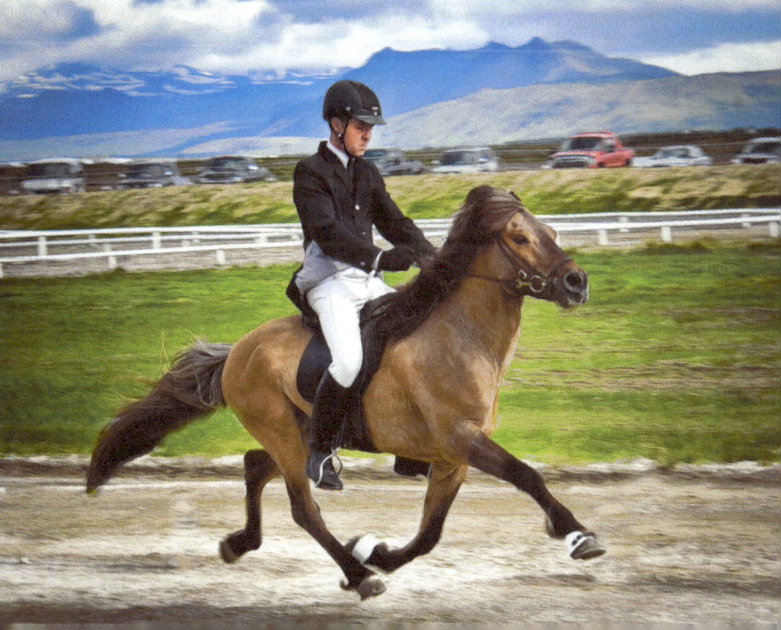

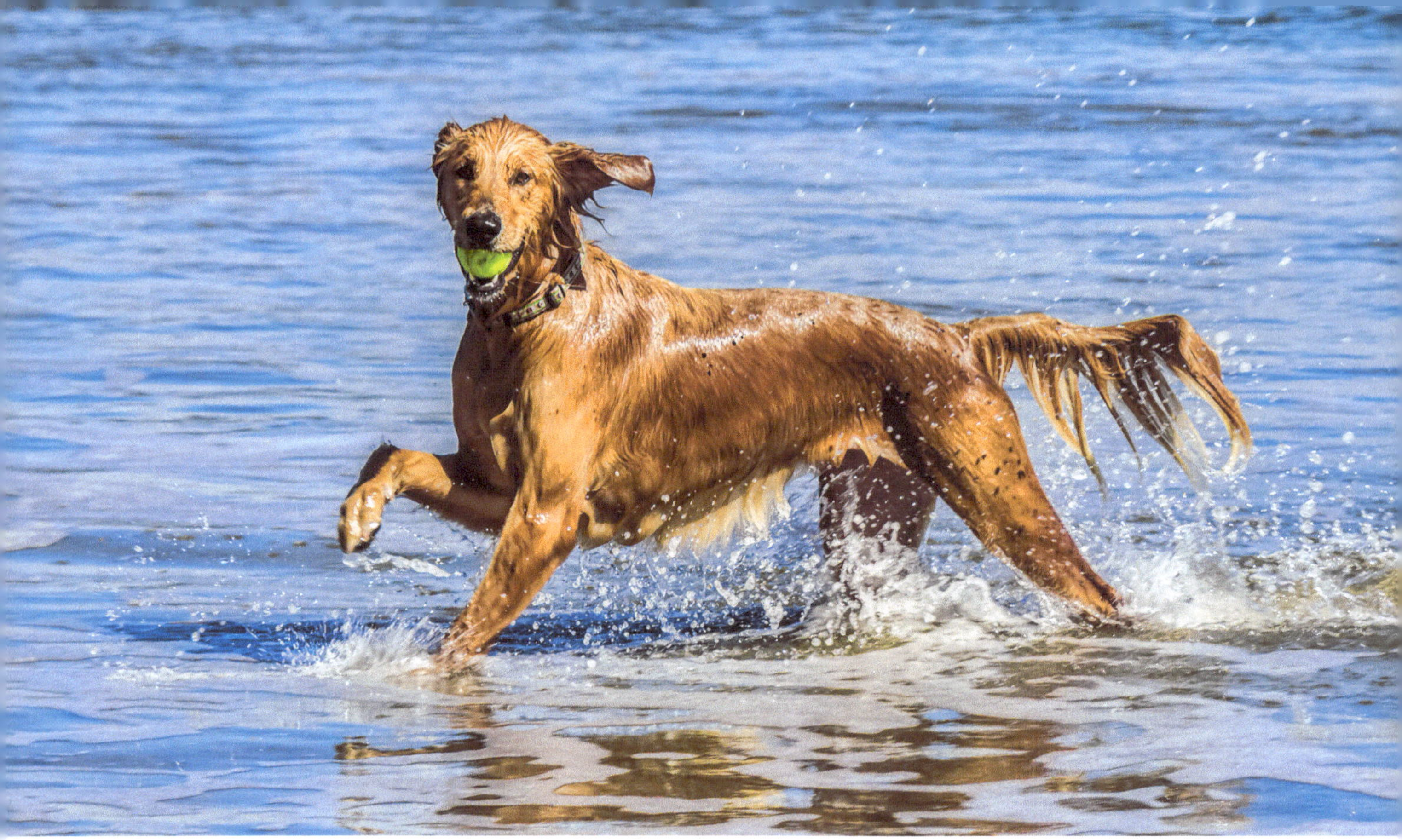

The photos on this spread were taken at Central California dog beaches.

Nothing is more uplifting than watching dogs frolic on the beach and in the ocean. Photographing them at play is fun and can create very dynamic images.

Targeting the motion at its peak is imperative.

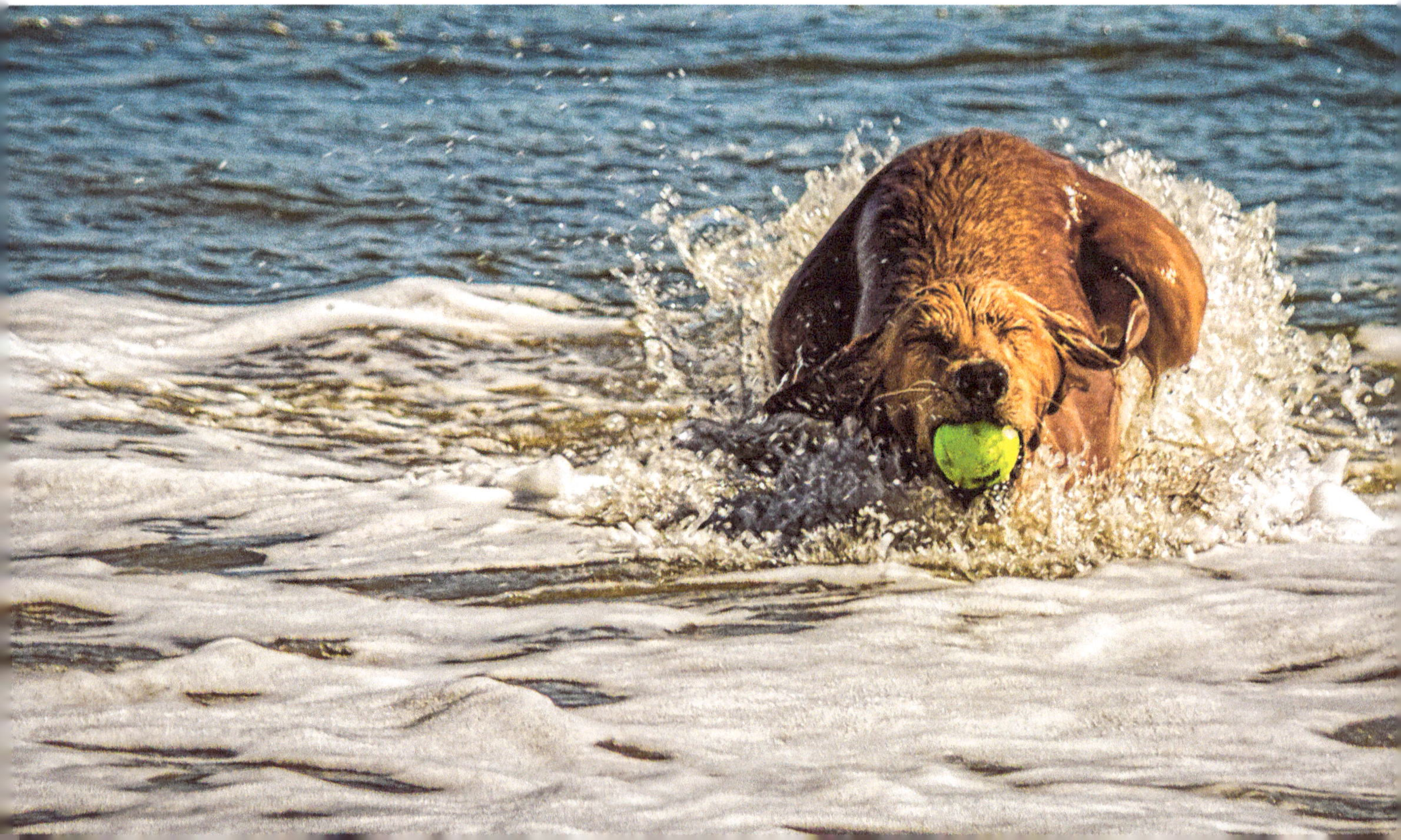

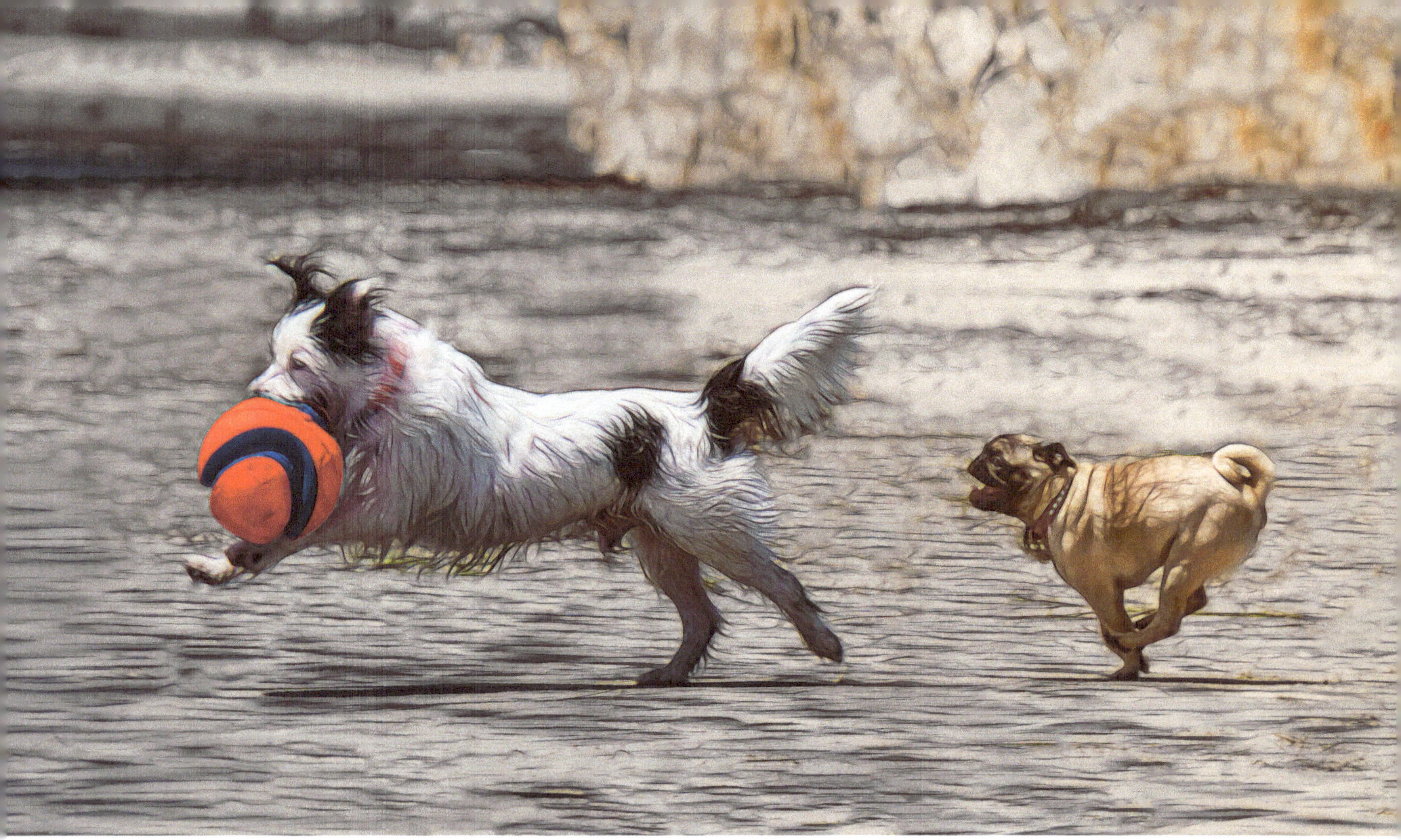

Most dogs walk, trot, and gallop, but some pace and single-foot.

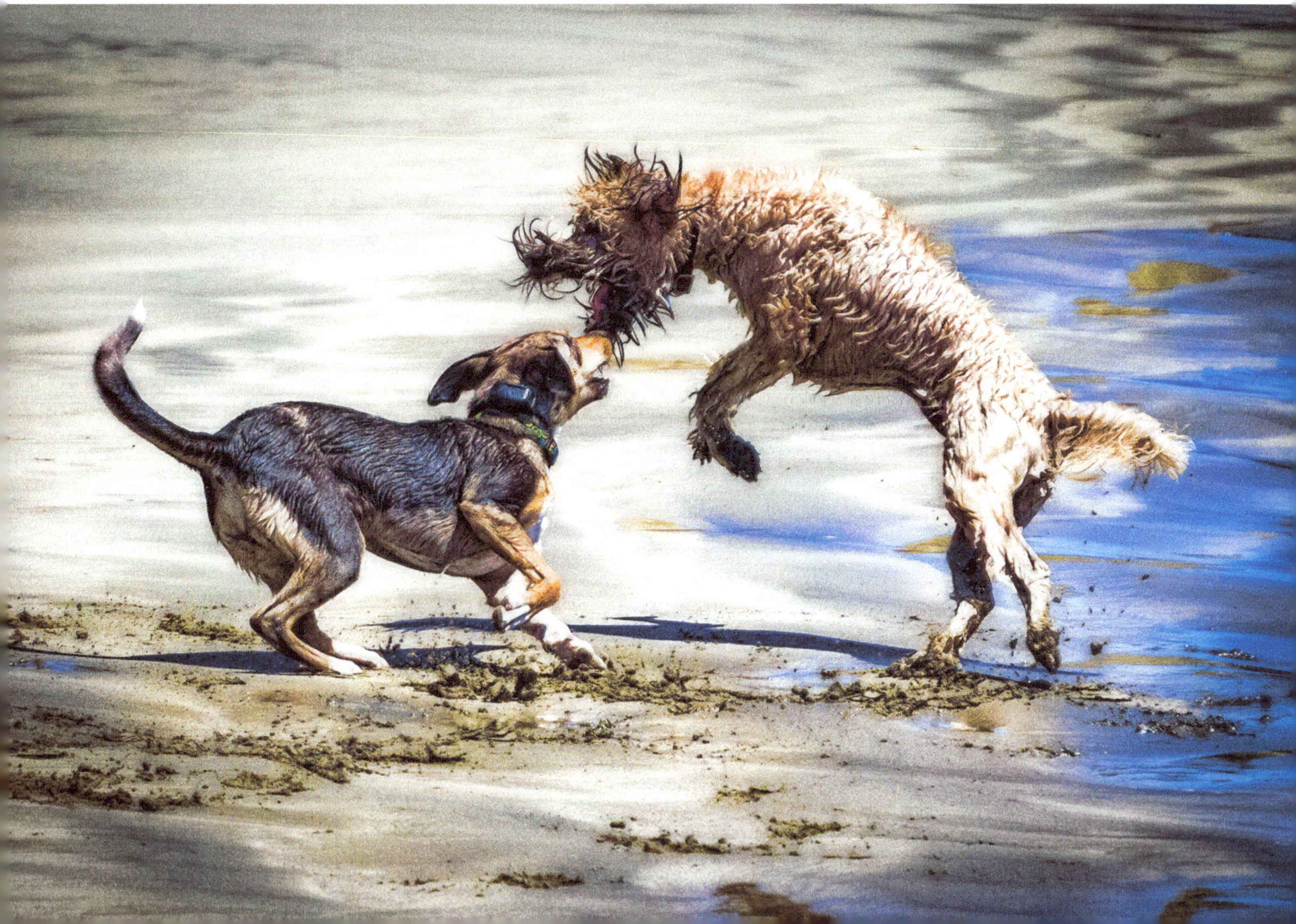

The flying patterns of birds vary according to type, species, and activity. Bigger, heavier birds have a harder time getting off the ground or water than smaller lighter birds. Each species of birds follow a set pattern, but no two species move in exactly the same way.

Water fowl generally skim across the water to gain speed before they can take off. Some birds fly solo. Others travel in large flocks.

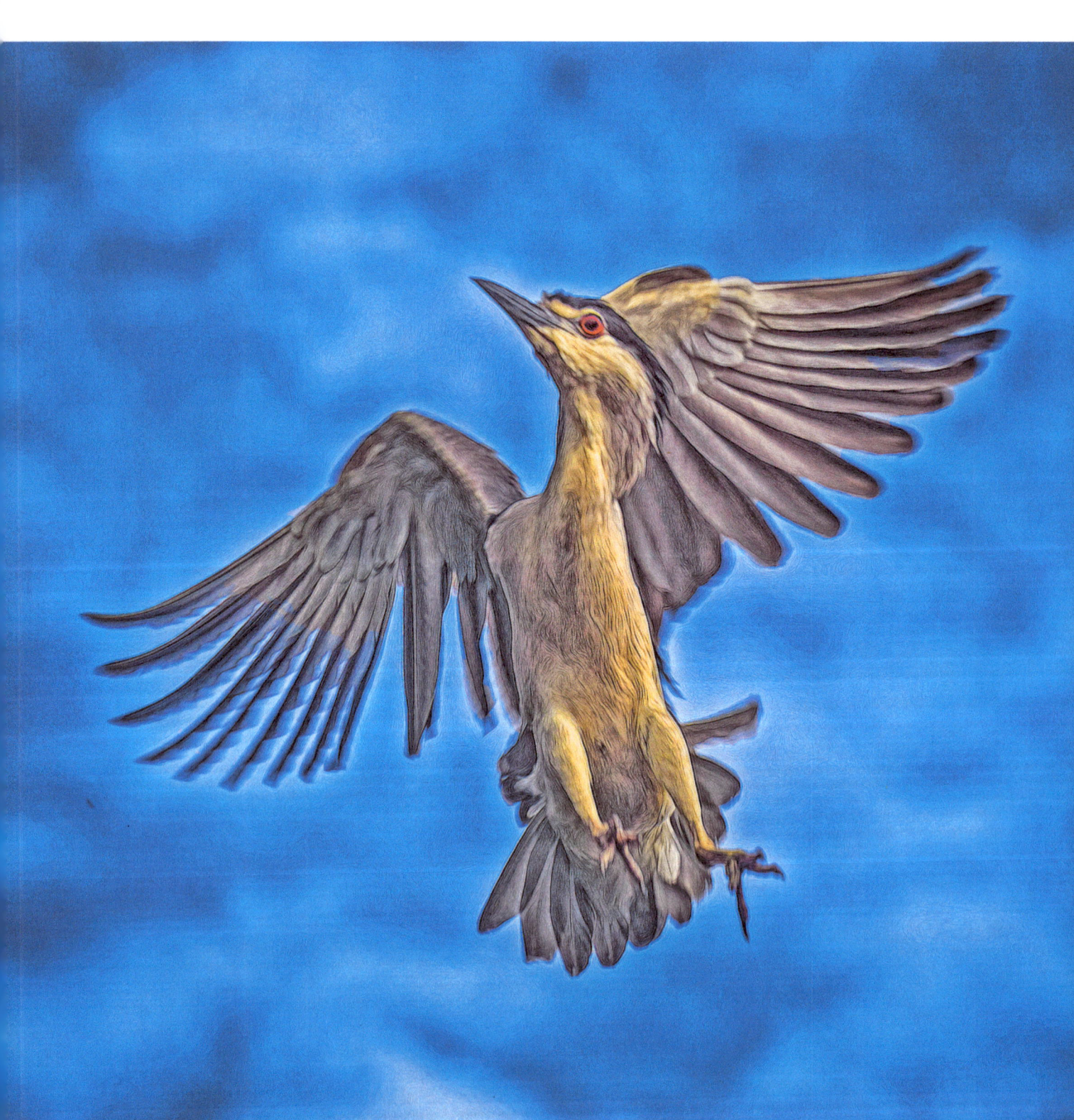

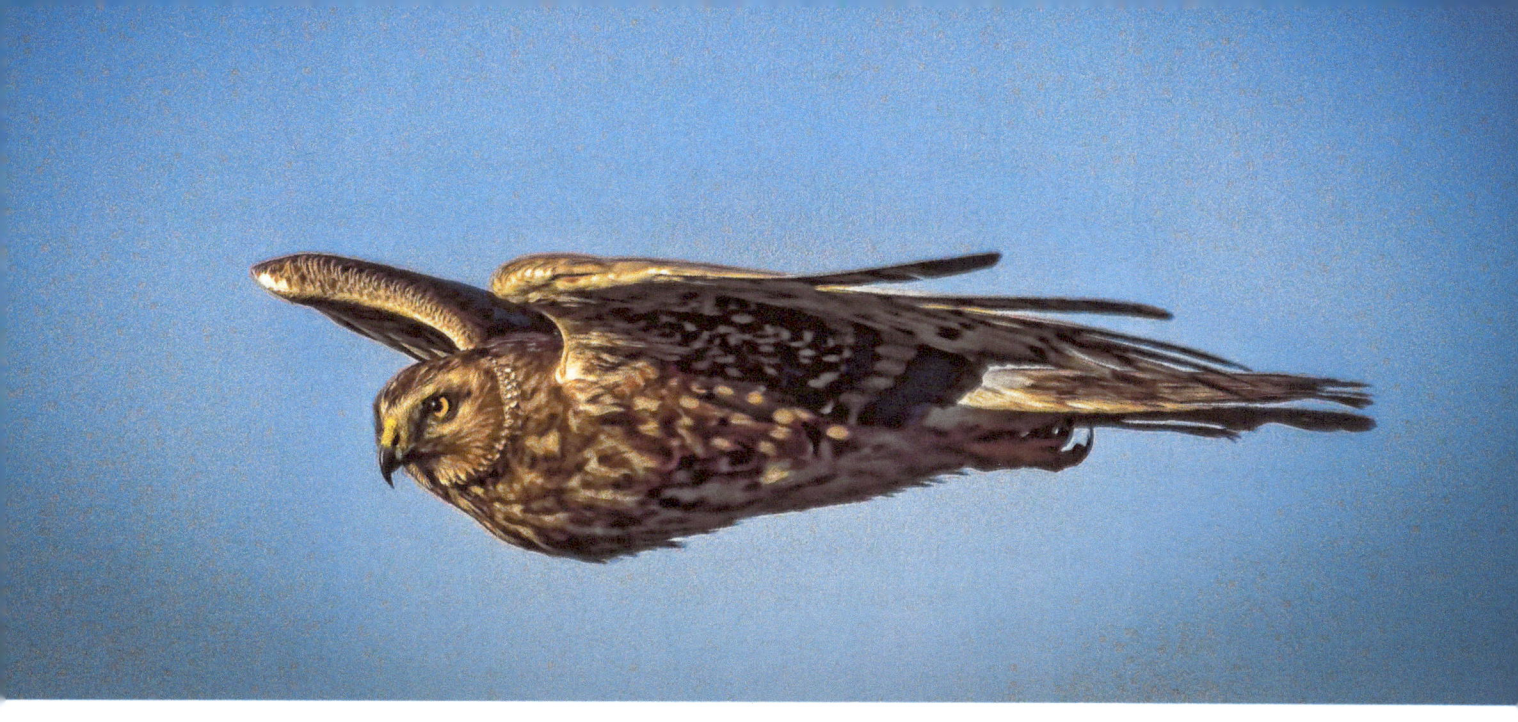

The Night Heron on the left page of the spread has just left its nest in a eucalyptus tree in search of food for its young. It is still trying to accelerate and gain height.

Hawks are difficult to get close to and shooting them in flight is tricky. I was able to get a series of clear, sharp shots of this one because it had young and was trying to draw my attention away from the nest.

The many birds in the photo below are terns gathered for a feeding frenzy. Assembled in a gigantic flock on the beach, they would all take off ever so often, only to return to the same spot a minute or two after.

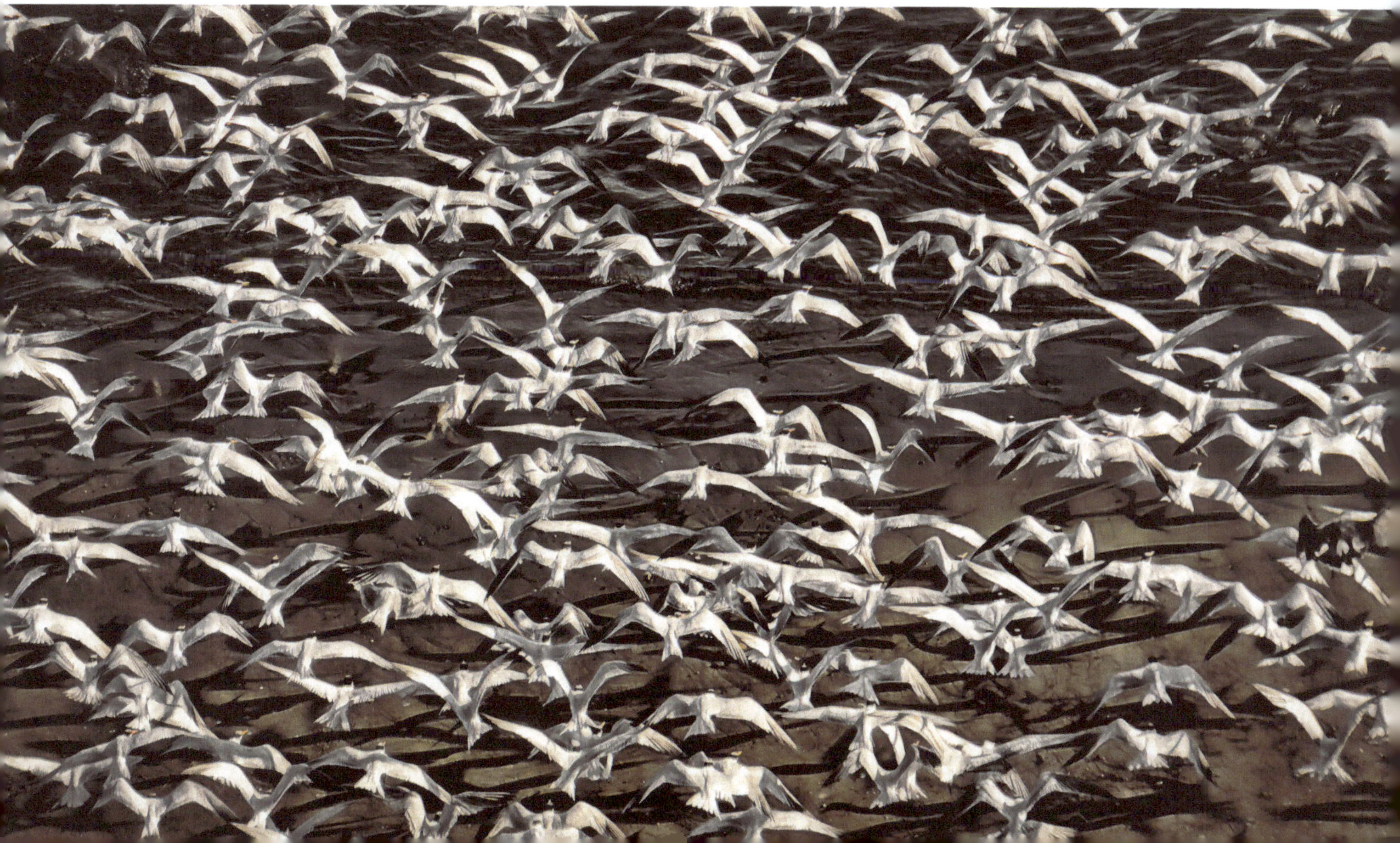

Watermark your photography by adding your personal point of view, your eye, your style, your voice, your soul, and your story to all of your images. Wear your heart on your sleeve. Be yourself. Be uniquely YOU!

Children in the Old West learned to shoot almost as soon as they were out of diapers. Those who practiced the most diligently—and kept on doing so—became the most accurate and the fastest on the draw. Today's police officers may never have to shoot anyone, yet they are required to target practice frequently.

Although photographers don't shoot with guns, target practice with cameras is of utmost importance if you want to consistently hit the mark. We all know how important it is to stay in shape and that practice makes perfect. Use every opportunity to photograph and take endless shots. Once you have taken all the action shots you feel you need, take five times more. Maybe you won't get any better exposures, but your reaction time will improve. It is a prerequisite, of course, that you shoot mindfully and keep focusing on doing your best.

Learn by doing! Try something new every day! Repetition is the mother of skill!

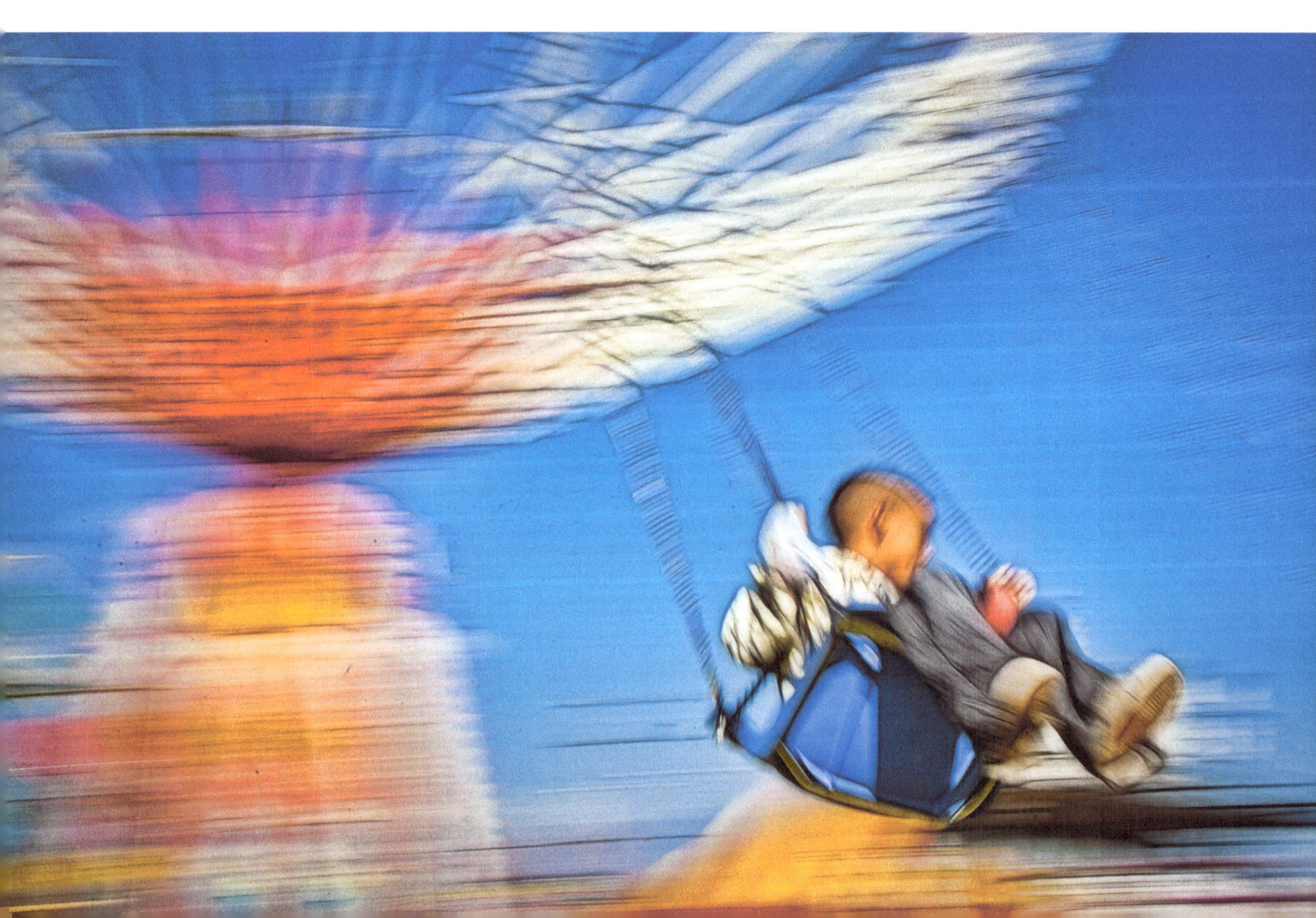

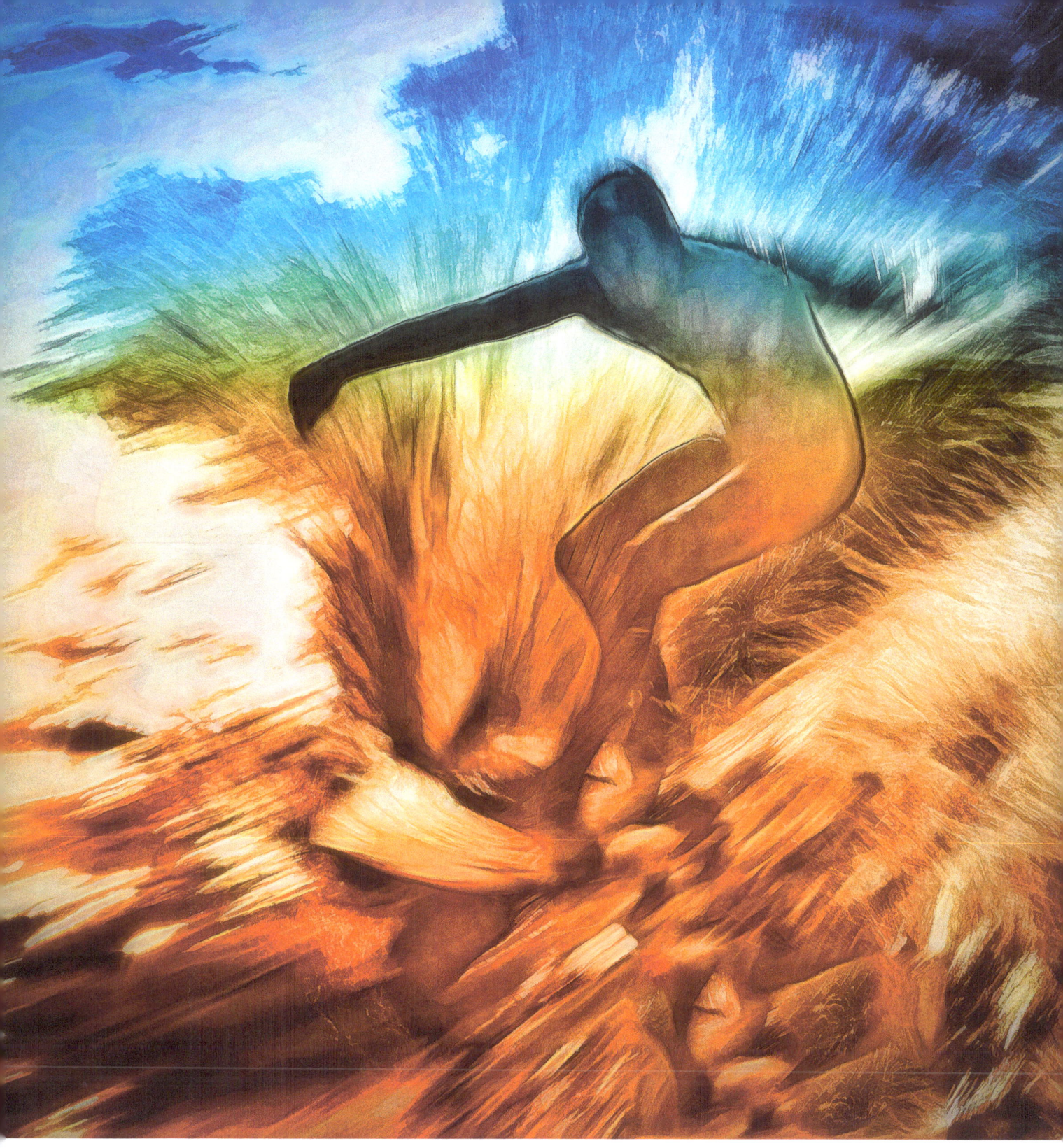

Both of the photos on this spread leap off the page. Both are experimental, colorful, and dynamic. Both have a distinct focus coupled with massive blur. Both images have a pleasing composition with the motion caught at its peak.

Think ahead! Be alert! Be prepared! Walk the extra mile! Train your muscle memory to react swiftly and precisely!

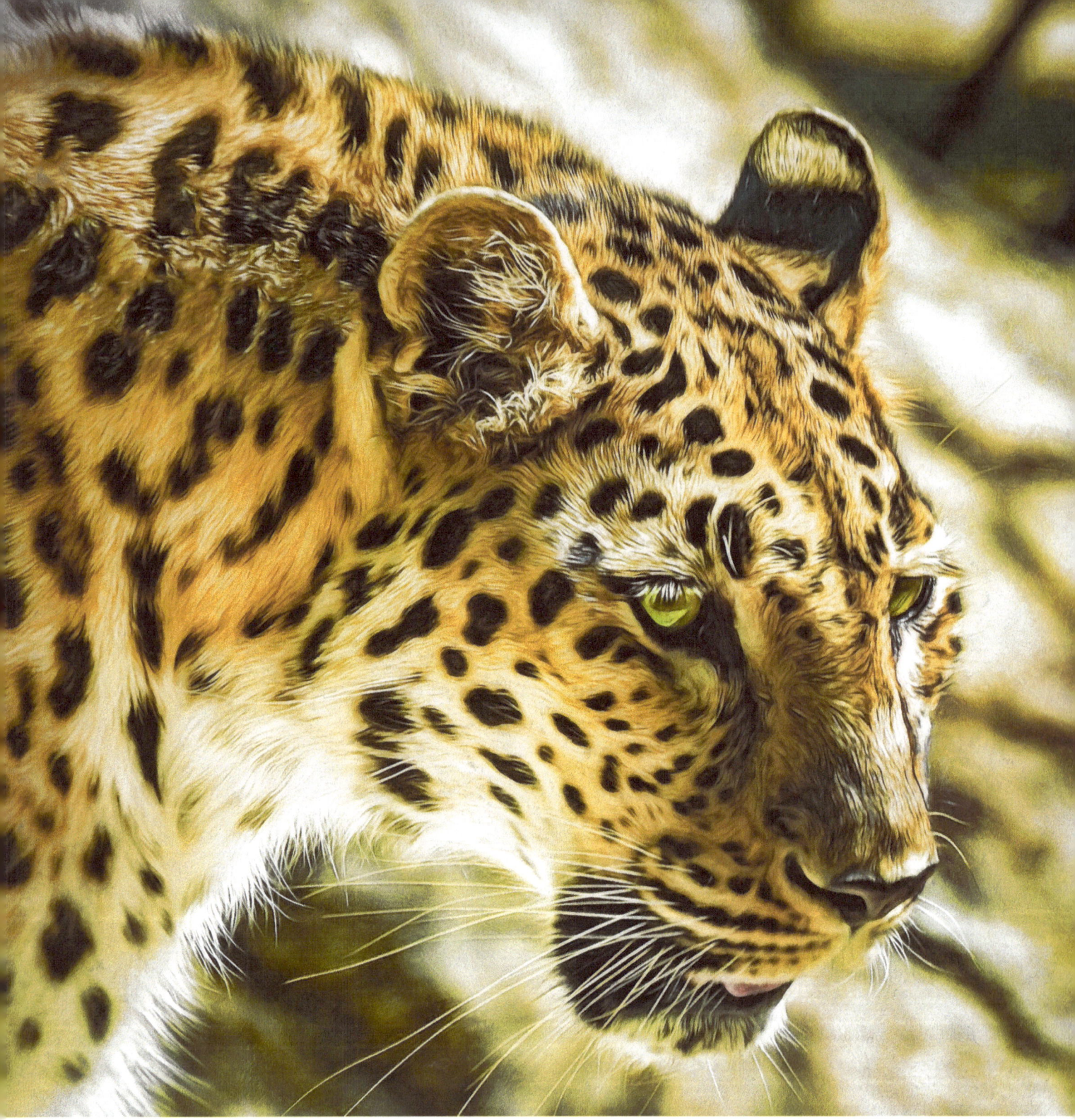

Photographic flow can appear to be a confusing concept. In reality it is quite simple. It is the directions and the speed of the viewer's eye traveling through the photograph. **Generally, the eye lands on the main point of interest.** Then it travels along a "cookie crumb trail" of actual or virtual leading lines through the pertinent points of the picture, slowing down as it passes them. Eliminate distractions. Use this spread as an example. Your eye will automatically land on the leopard's eye. From here it travels on an imaginary straight line to the deer's hind leg. From here it follows a line to its head.

Whatever you hunt will try to elude you. Whatever you attract will come to you. This is as true of amazing photos as of everything else.

Whenever you embark on a photo shoot, consider making your goal to seek new knowledge—to learn. In the long run, doing so will serve you better than focusing on competing with everyone else for the best shot. Your skills improve with the added understanding you gain. And by seeking rather than hunting, you will put yourself in a state of mind that attracts great shots rather than repels them.

Prey animals have their eyes on the side of their face giving them wide vision and the ability to see a great range of what is going on around them. Predators have their eyes in front of their head. This gives them the narrow point of view they need to hunt—focus on their prey, only.

Prey animals instinctively know that predators are only dangerous when they are hungry. When we put a camera in front of our face we look like predators and our point of view narrows. We automatically snap into hunt mode. Unless we revise our state of mind—animals and people alike—automatically view us as hungry one eyed predators and move away.

The trick to engaging our photographic subjects is to consciously soften our state of mind and our body language. We need to feel like flight animals or sated predators. And we need to appear as such to others. Also, when we are in prey—rather than predator mode—our field of vision widens. This allows us to notice a myriad of movement we otherwise would have missed.

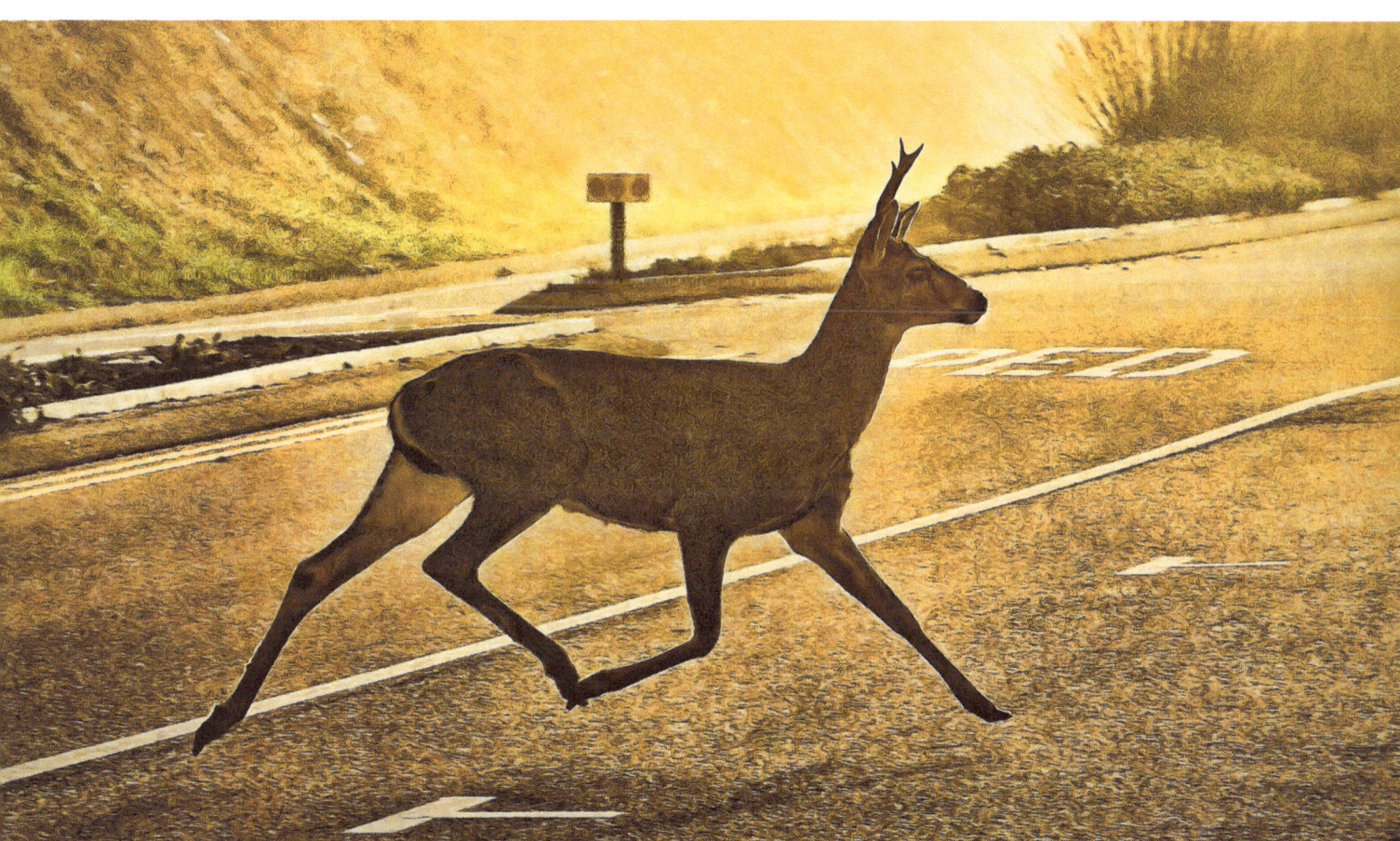

Let your photos come to you. Soften your eye, relax your body language, widen your vision, and enjoy yourself.

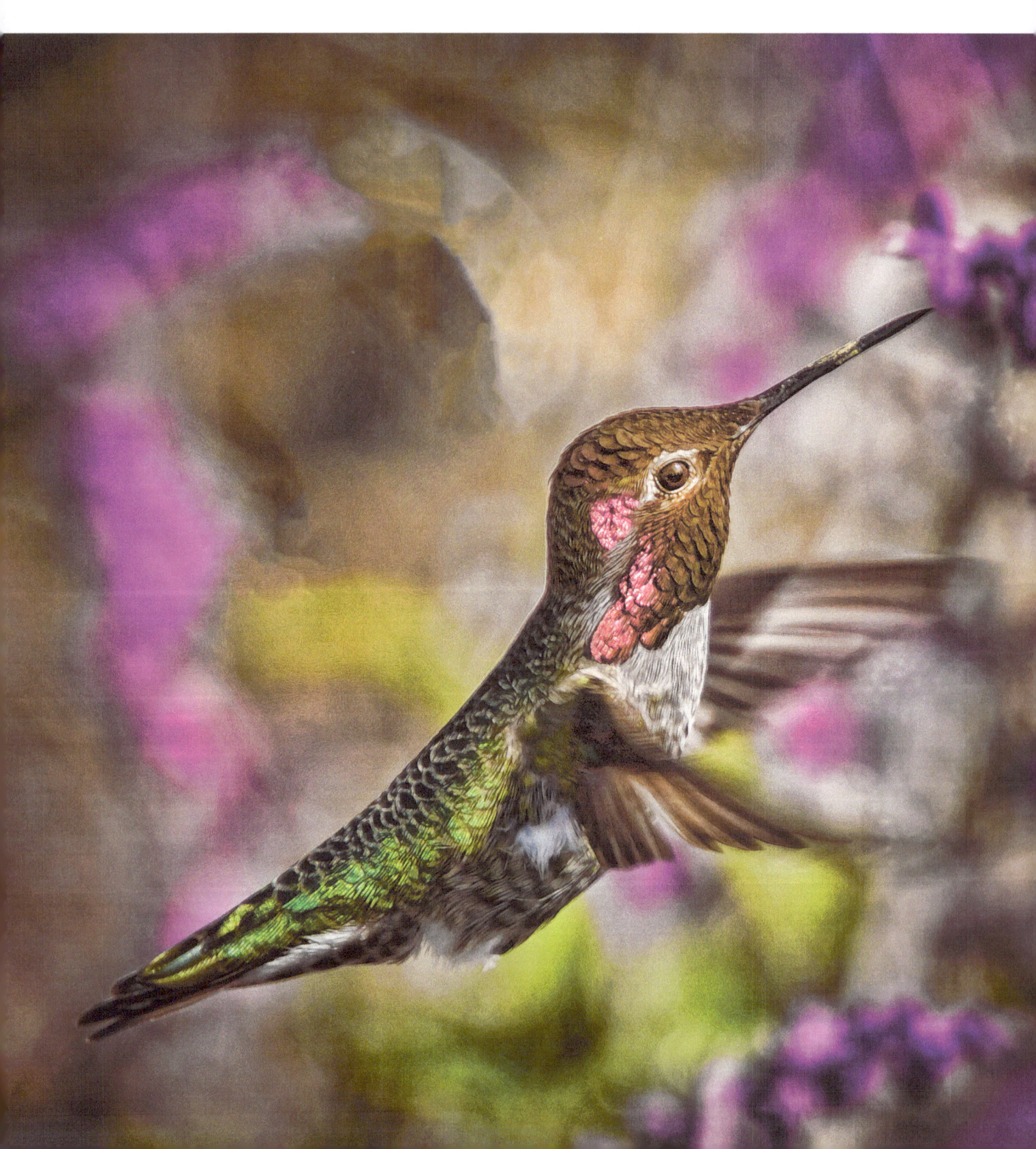

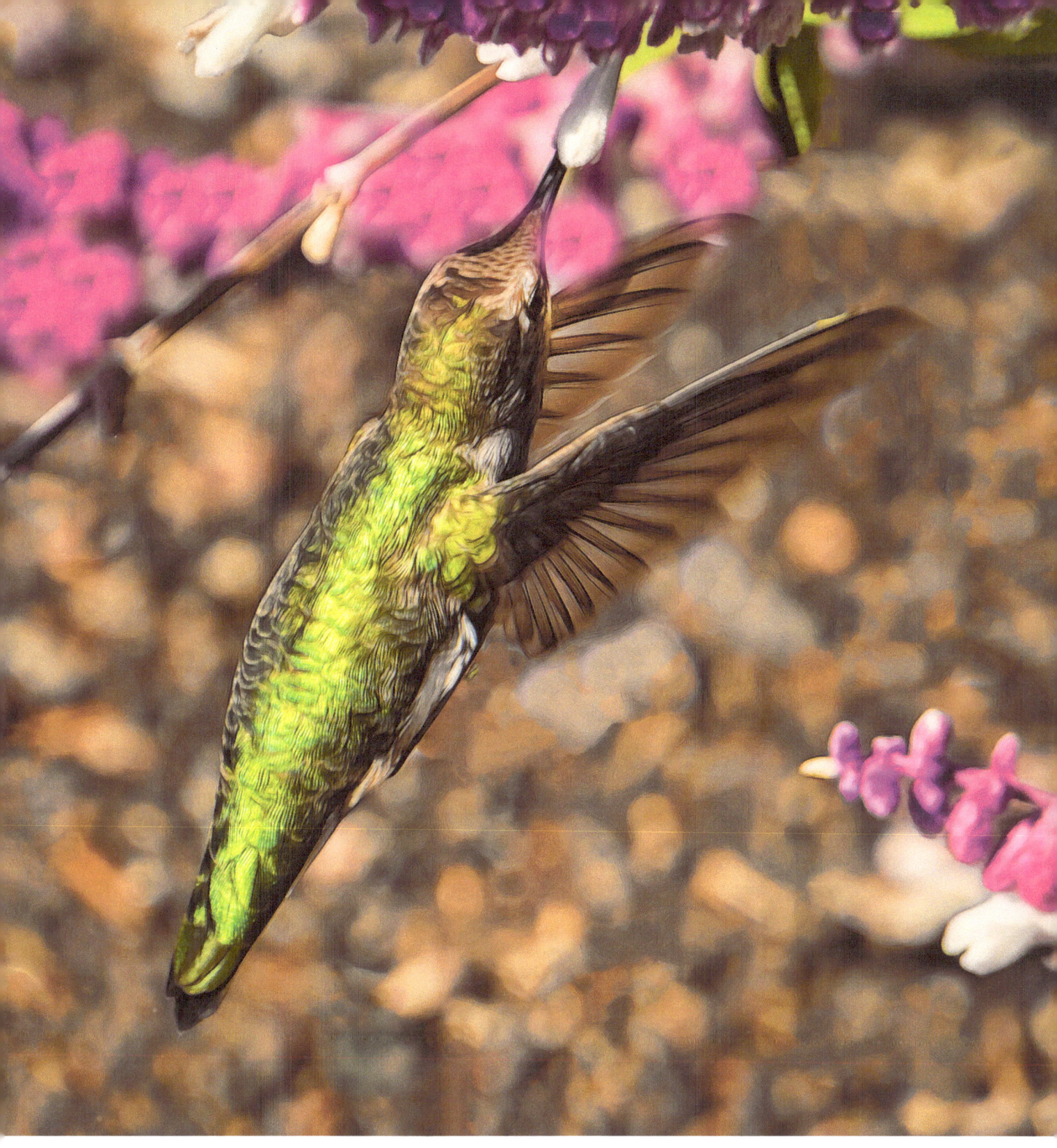

You need to know a rule before you can break it!

Learning is creating a connection between the unknown and what you already know.

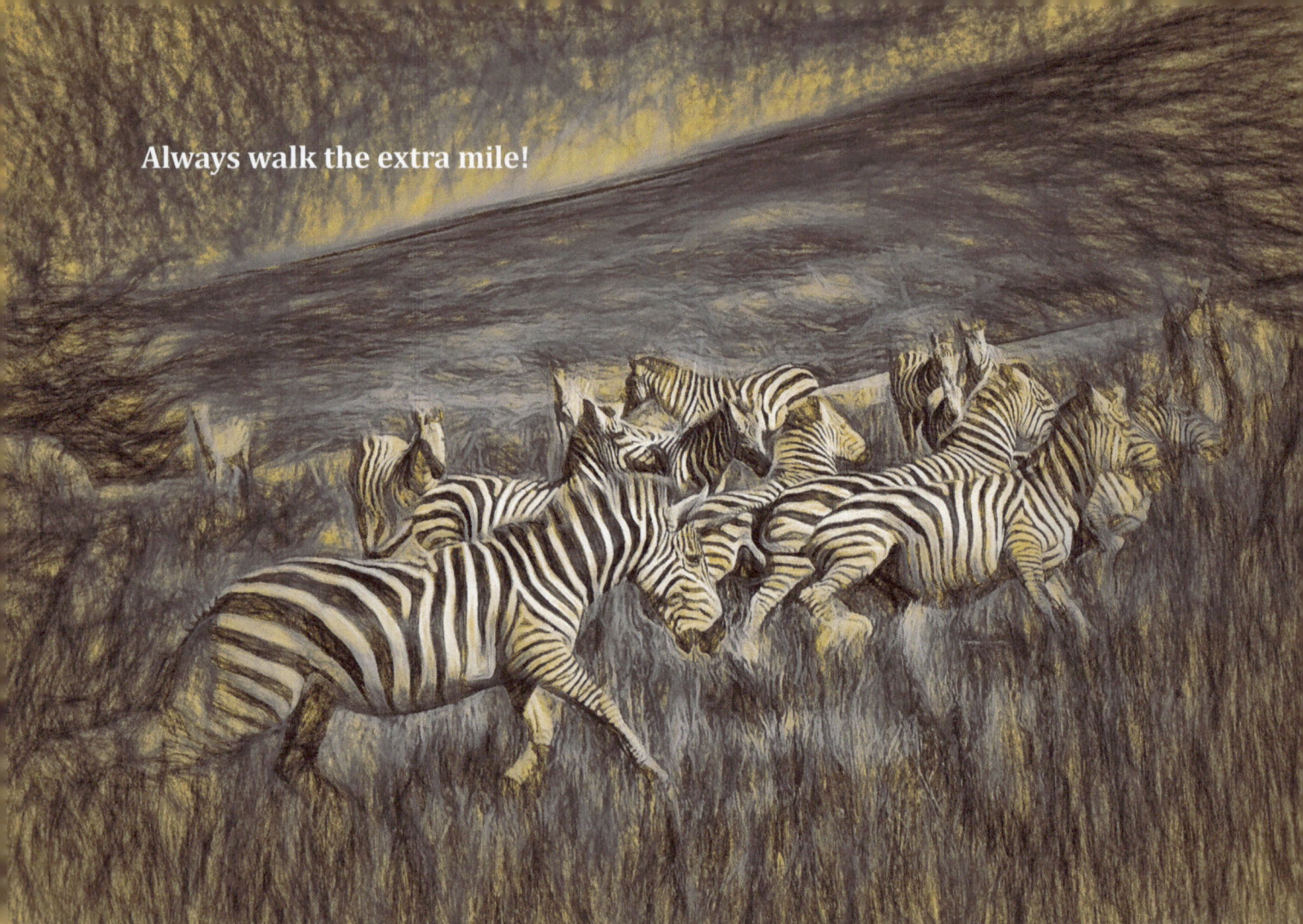

Always walk the extra mile!

Nowadays, enhancing your photos using software filters is a fun and resourceful activity . By doing so, you can achieve amazing results. The process jump starts your creative juices and it allows you to view photography from a totally different point of view.

Nonetheless—if you are serious about your art—don't settle for less. Rather than push a button or two in some cheesy iPhone app just because you can, download trial versions of some of the more advanced filters. Each brand creates different results. Some software designers are more sophisticated. Others are more in your face. Neither is right or wrong. Choose what appeals to you.

Don't mess with your photos just because you feel you should. Have a plan! Envision the result you want to create and figure out how to achieve it. Mix and match, but use the filters at full strength only in exceptional cases. Find the fade slider in the software you have chosen and use it diligently.

Keep your vision in mind and stick to it. Don't let yourself get overwhelmed by the many choices. And don't let yourself get distracted by some cool effect or the other. Each time you have pushed a button, evaluate the result. Then ask yourself whether that step got you closer to your goal or moved you further away from it. If you did not get closer to what you want, try something else.

The zebras on the left page of the spread are a part of the Hearst Ranch herd. Passing by one day, I was fortunate enough to catch them in a momentous playing spree. Highway One immediately became a virtual traffic jam as I—and almost everybody else—pulled over to photograph them from where Cal Trans has bulldozed a gigantic turnout.

*What always amazes me when I stop to photograph the zebras is that most of the others who do so barely get out of the cars. Whereas they take the time to position themselves and/or the family, in front of their cameras, they do not worry about getting as close to the action as they can by walking the fifty feet to the fence. **Get as close to the action as you can!***

The lions below were one of my magic zoo moments. I no longer remember at which park it was. I believe what makes this image a success is the strong leading lines and the circular movement of the leaping lions.

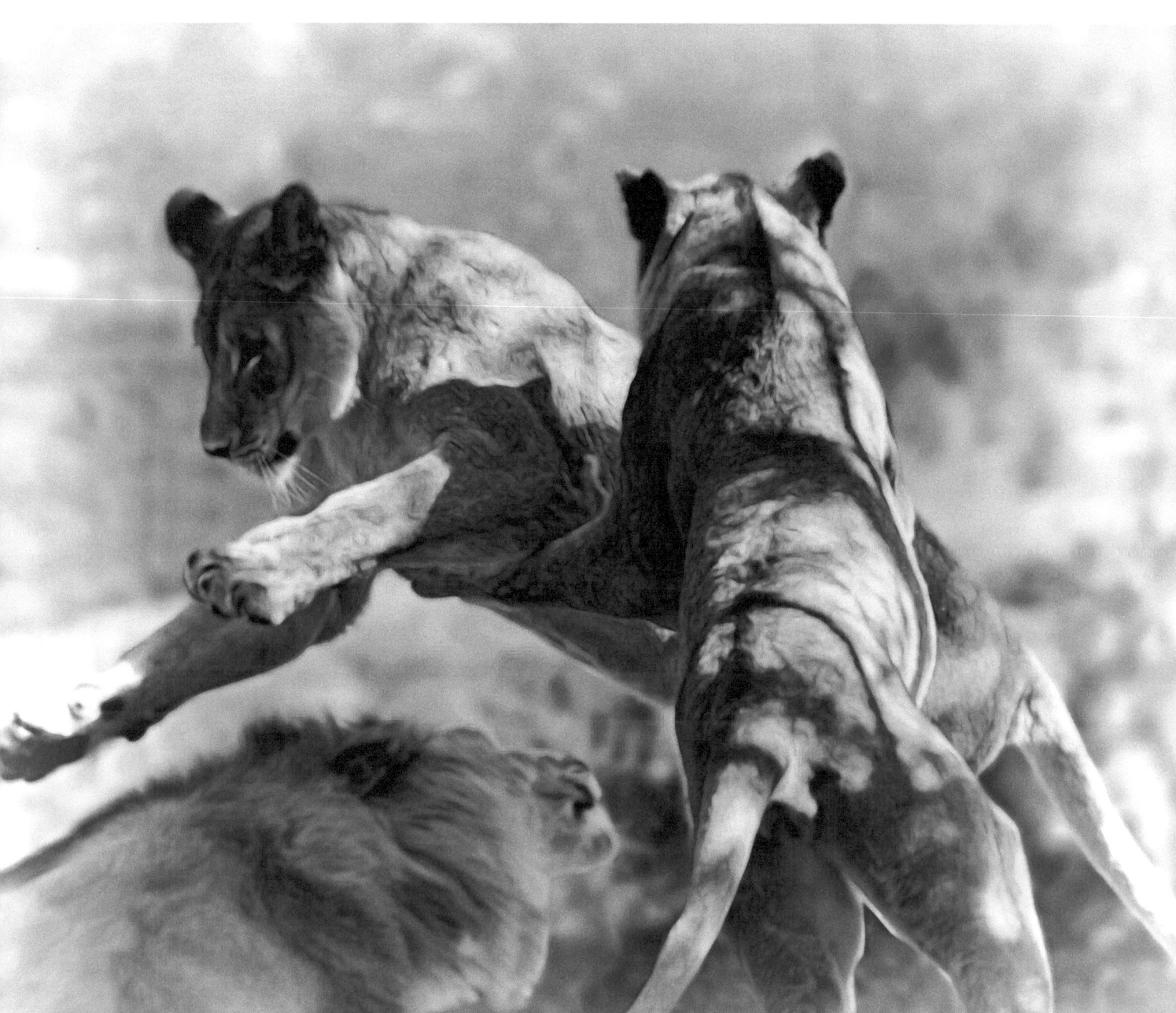

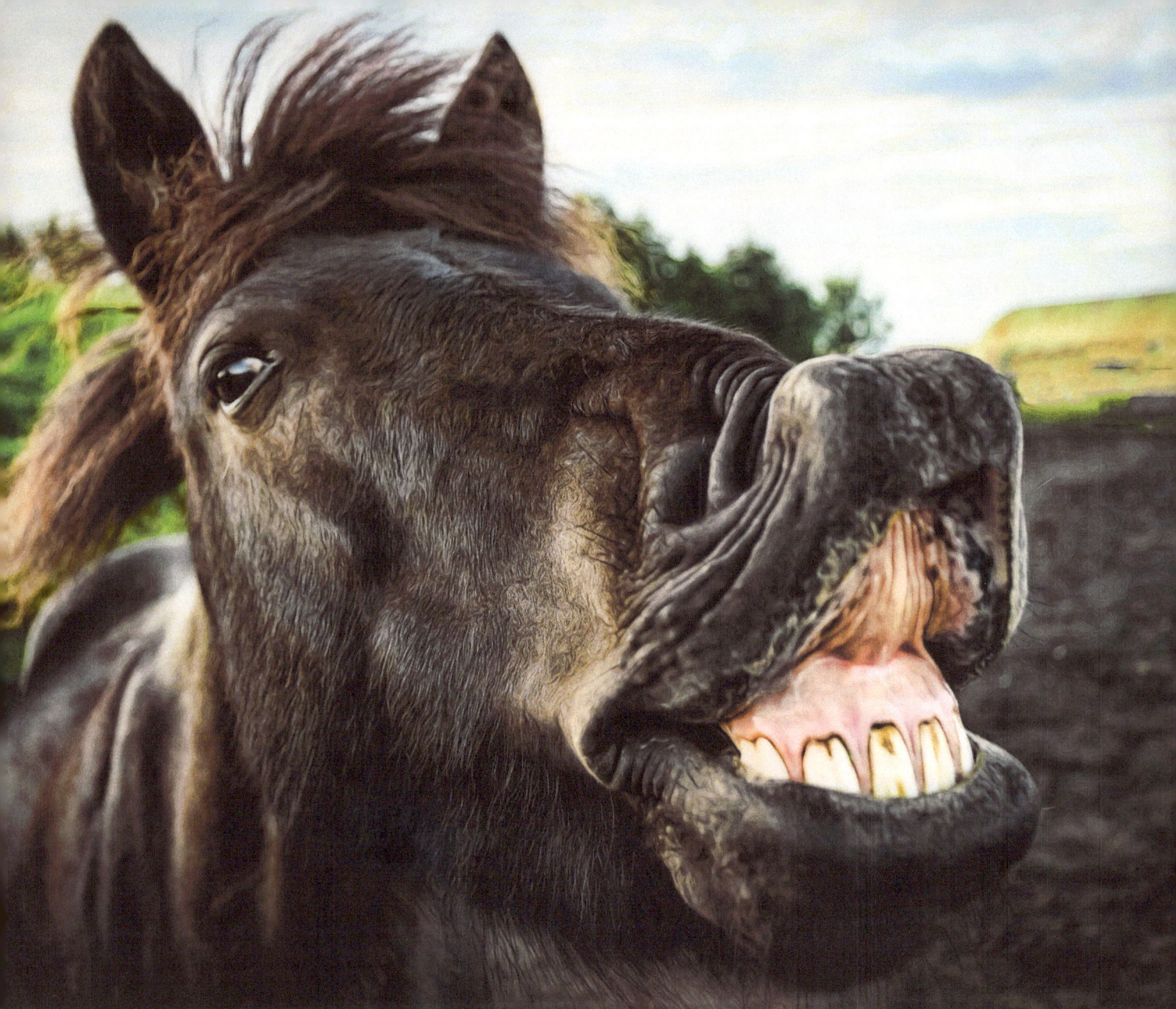

What I like most about the photos on this spread is their fun and spontaneity. I took the photo on this page in Iceland. Some might argue that it isn't an action shot, but I beg to differ. Without the eye contact and the drastic movement of the horse's mouth the image would merely be another horse head caricature.

The photo to the right is from a fun photo shoot I did at my friend Kimberly's ranch in San Diego. Most likely our original intent was merely to get the jumping horse in the picture. But by including Kimberly in the picture, I definitely added to the story. A just ho-hum photo suddenly became funny.

The motion flows pleasantly, both horse and human are in balance, and the action was recorded almost at its peak moment.

What friends do you have that you can play with and use as fun photo models?

Straight from the horse's mouth:

Lead rather than follow.
Aim for the stars!
Hang loose!
Have fun!
Shoot with passion!
Be trigger happy and fast on the draw.
Imagine, envision, experiment!
Come from the heart!
Be yourself!
Don't be afraid that others might think you silly or inferior!
Think strategy! Be precise.
Target practice and when in doubt, shoot!

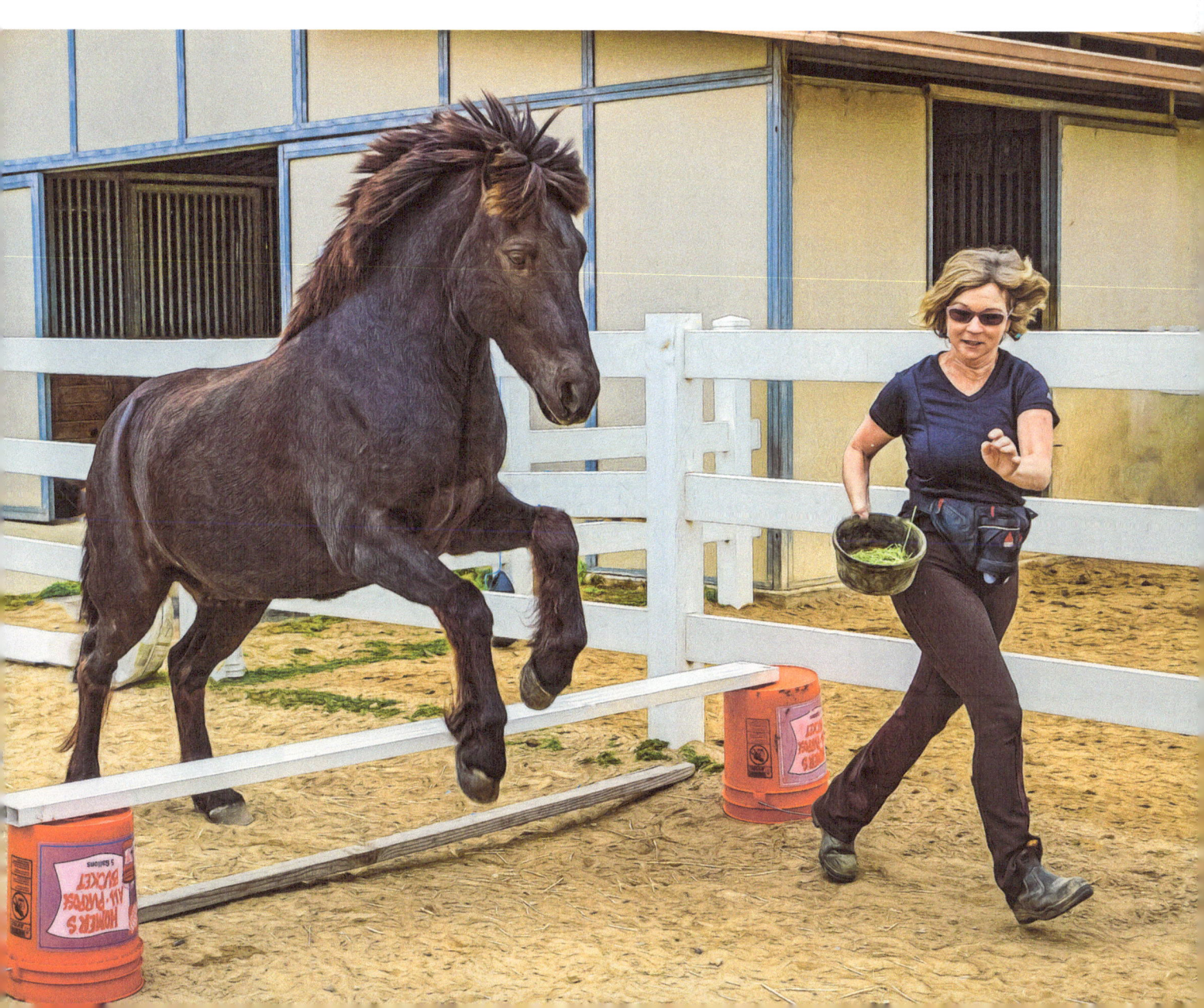

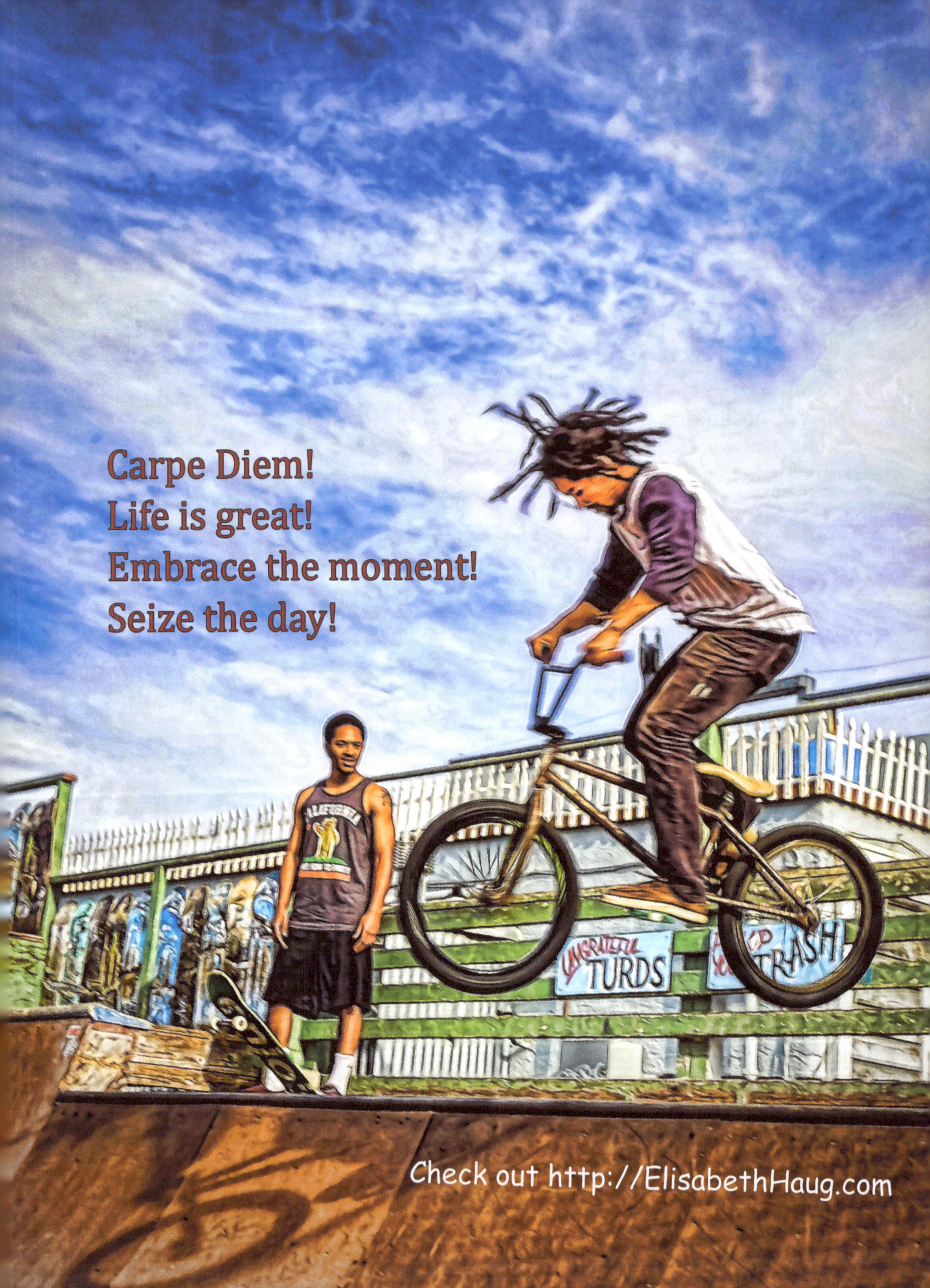

Carpe Diem!
Life is great!
Embrace the moment!
Seize the day!

Check out http://ElisabethHaug.com